7 Charting Tools for Spread Betting

A practical guide to making money from spread betting with technical analysis

by Malcolm Pryor

HARRIMAN HOUSE LTD

3A Penns Road
Petersfield
Hampshire
GU32 2EW
GREAT BRITAIN

Tel: +44 (0)1730 233870
Fax: +44 (0)1730 233880
Email: enquiries@harriman-house.com
Website: www.harriman-house.com

First published in Great Britain in 2009 by Harriman House.

978-1-905641-84-0

British Library Cataloguing in Publication Data
A CIP catalogue record for this book can be obtained from the British Library.

Printed in the UK by CPI William Clowes, Beccles NR34 7TL

For Karen

Contents

About the author

Malcolm Pryor is an active spread bettor and investor, a trading coach, and the author of two previous books on spread betting, *The Financial Spread Betting Handbook* and *Winning Spread Betting Strategies*. He is also the author and presenter of the DVD *Malcolm Pryor on Short Term Spread Betting*.

He comments regularly on spread betting issues and on the markets at www.spreadbettingcentral.co.uk, and runs training seminars on spread betting (details at www.sparkdales.co.uk).

He is a member of the Society of Technical Analysts in the UK and has been designated a Certified Financial Technician by the International Federation of Technical Analysts.

He is an expert at several games, including bridge where he has held the rank of Grandmaster or higher for over a decade.

Preface

What this book covers

In this book I explain seven technical analysis tools which can really make a difference to spread betting performance. The seven tools covered are:

1. ATR

2. Directional movement

3. Moving averages

4. Support and resistance

5. Oscillators

6. Relative strength

7. Momentum

The focus is on practical use rather than academic theory. So I show how each tool can help improve performance and how to use it to best effect. There are many charts in this book illustrating each tool. Each tool has its own individual role to play in the trader's methodology, either on its own or in combination with some of the other tools.

Who this book is for

The book is for people with any level of technical analysis skills, from virtual beginners to advanced users. The beginner may want to supplement their reading by reading various free online resources referred to in the text. All readers are also referred to further research by way of a recommended reading list.

Although the book is primarily for spread bettors it is not necessary for the reader to have any previous spread betting experience, the concepts discussed are of potential interest to all traders.

The focus of the book is mostly on daily charts, and as such will be of interest to traders whose trades last from a couple of days to say 30 days. However the tools can be applied to all time frames. So the day trader can use the basic principles on, say, a 10 minute chart, while the longer-term investor can use the basic principles on weekly charts.

How this book is structured

After this preface there is a short introduction – the main purpose of which is to explain the reasons for writing this book.

Then we get to the heart of the book. Each of the seven charting tools is explained in a separate chapter, all of which have the same structure:

1. **Background and construction.** Each chapter starts with a brief introduction, followed by a first look at the tool in action, illustrated most of the time with an annotated chart of the FTSE 100. This leads on to a detailed look at how the tool in constructed. In a number of cases the more complicated arithmetic can be found in the Appendices.

2. **Overview of tool.** In this section we look at the main purpose of the tool, its strengths and its weaknesses.

3. **Settings.** For each tool where the user has a choice of settings we look at both the standard settings and the ones used in this book.

4. **How to use this tool.** This section focuses on how the tool is used in this book.

5. **Example.** Each chapter contains a detailed worked example of the tool in action.

6. **Alternatives.** In some cases the user can get similar benefits from other tools, which are discussed here.

7. **Conclusion.** Each chapter finishes with a very brief final comment on the tool.

Following this there is a chapter on how the tools can be combined to build, or complement, a trading methodology.

Finally, the Appendix lists books and internet resources that I recommend as useful for spread bettors, and also provides further notes on the detailed calculations of the indicators.

Acknowledgements

I have many people to thank for providing support advice and encouragement while writing this book. I shall not be able to name them all – but many thanks everyone!

I would like to thank Harriman House for their help in publishing this book; a really great team. In particular, Stephen Eckett, who provides unique editorial wisdom with a light touch.

I would like to take this opportunity to thank Martin Stamp, the creator of the ShareScope software, and the entire ShareScope team, both for creating the software and for allowing me to reproduce charts from it in this book.

I would like to thank Dr Van Tharp, friend and mentor.

I would like to thank my parents, Maurice, who passed away in 2008, and Marjorie.

And most of all I would like to thank Karen, to whom this book is dedicated.

Risk warning

No responsibility for loss incurred by any person or corporate body acting or refraining to act as a result of reading material in this book can be accepted by the Publisher or the Author.

The information provided by the Author is not offered as, nor should it be inferred to be, advice or recommendation to readers, since the financial circumstances of readers will vary greatly and investment or trading behaviour which may be appropriate for one reader is unlikely to be appropriate for others.

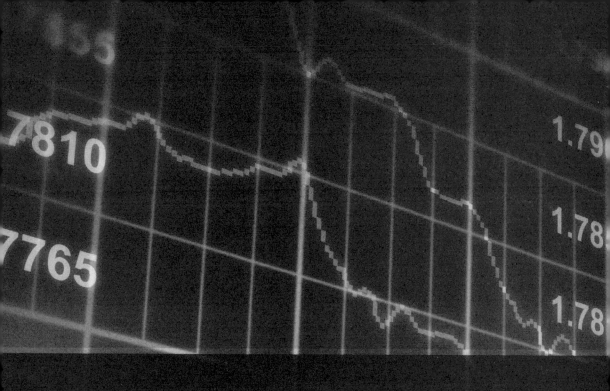

INTRODUCTION

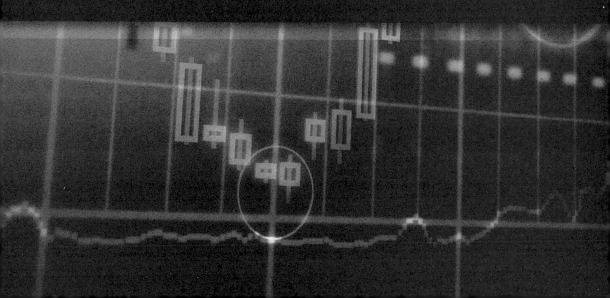

Introduction

Spread betting using a structured approach

My first book looked at the differences between people who win at spread betting and those that don't. One of the big differences is that the winners use a structured approach. They plan their trades and use systems and techniques that in the long run give them an edge. They also keep their bet size at a level which will give their longer-term edge a chance to play out while still keeping them in the game during the inevitable shorter-term volatility.

In the winner's enclosure you find a surprisingly large number of diverse approaches. Some people perform detailed analysis of company results, poring over balance sheets, profit and loss statements, cash flow schedules and the like. Others have expertise in strategic planning, marketing and sales, and can spot a company that seems to be going places. Others have corporate finance skills and try to make money by guessing the next takeover target.

The technical analysis community believe that the study of price action alone can provide an edge – that certain patterns of price movement have predictive value which can be exploited.

In my view technical analysis is ideally suited for spread betting, where one can bet on short-term price movements with leverage, and where part of the game is identifying logical places to enter and exit a bet.

Which technical analysis tools to select?

The difficulty facing many spread bettors is that there is a vast array of technical analysis tools available, many of which are now easily accessible either via the spread betting firms themselves or through third party trading and investment software, including many free online services. For most spread bettors the process of selecting which technical analysis tools to use is largely a matter of trial and (expensive) error.

So many parameters...

Even after selecting potentially useful tools, the spread bettor is then faced with a multitude of choices about which parameters to use on the selected tools. Once again this often involves further research, time and money.

The reason for this book

I like to focus on a relatively small number of technical analysis tools which I have learnt how to use in a way that helps me. I get so many questions on this that I thought it might help others if I documented how I use various tools. This book is about the technical analysis tools which I believe give me an edge and the parameters I use for them.

Background information

Before we start I want to talk briefly about:

- charting software, and

- technical analysis concepts.

1. Charting software

This book uses ShareScope software to illustrate the tools we look at. I have used the software for many years and all my books have featured it. I like it.

If you don't have ShareScope you will find that you can get access to many of the tools in this book through free sites on the internet. I personally don't find this route as convenient (and so I am prepared to pay both for the convenience and for the full functionality of the ShareScope software), but the free sites may work for you. Try the following:

www.uk.finance.yahoo.com

www.money.uk.msn.com

www.advfn.com

www.digitallook.com

Alternative suppliers of software you have to pay for include:

www.equis.com (Metastock)

www.esignal.com

www.simplychart.com

www.trackdata.com

This is far from an exhaustive list. If you search the internet for investment software or trading software you will find more suppliers.

The spread betting firms themselves also supply technical analysis functionality, but the quality varies quite a bit, and often the data is based on the firms' own prices rather than the underlying market.

2. Technical analysis concepts

I have written this book so that it can be read both by people with very little prior knowledge of technical analysis and by seasoned technical analysis practitioners. I try to explain the various concepts in each chapter but there are one or two which deserve a comment up front.

User defined

You will come across the expression "user defined" quite a bit in the text. For example, in "user defined number of periods". What this means is that typically there are a number of different settings which traders favour when using the tool, and that typically the software allows the user of the software to alter these parameters according to preference.

Take for instance the indicator RSI which we will be having a look at: the standard setting for this indicator is 14 days, but you should be able to change this on your software to another number.

What number?

Well, that's for later...

Fractals

A nice name for quite a simple phenomenon. A three bar pattern, which comprises either:

- a bar with a low that is lower than the bar on either side of it, or

- a bar with a high that is higher than the bar on either side of it.

In the first case that low represents the point at which the bears were no longer able to push prices lower, and if price comes back to that point again, maybe they will fail to push prices lower again.

In the second case that high represents the point at which the bulls were no longer able to push prices higher, and if price comes back to that point again, maybe they will fail again at that point to push prices higher.

I explain this some more in the text, but I mention it up front because for me it is one of the most powerful trading concepts I know.

In the literature these points are often named differently (e.g. pivot points) but I like fractal.

Further research

Various online resources are recommended if you want to research the topics in this book further and an extensive reading list is in the Appendix.

There is a great site, www.stockcharts.com, which has a good, free instructional area.

And you can consult with the user community of www.spreadbettingcentral.co.uk by posting on the forum there.

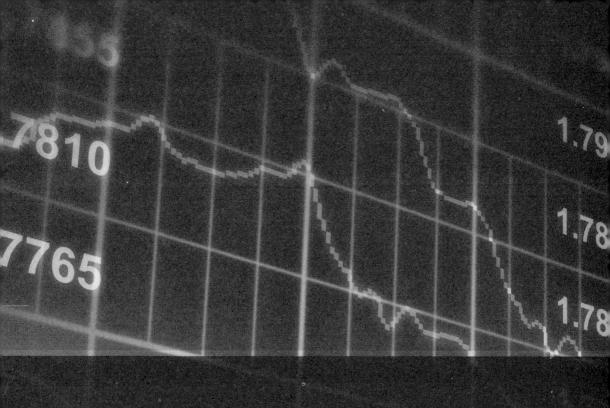

THE SEVEN TOOLS

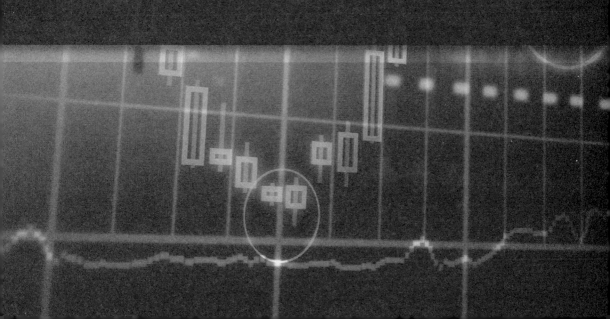

TOOL 1: ATR

Background and construction

ATR is one of a number of indicators which measure volatility. Volatility can be described as a measure of the state of instability. In trading, volatility is a measure of the instability of the price of a financial instrument. Traders need some volatility in the financial instruments they trade, for without it there would be no price movement to take advantage of. Having a tool to measure volatility allows the trader to adapt to varying volatility, for instance by having wider stops when volatility increases and tighter stops when volatility decreases.

ATR is short for Average True Range, a concept described by Welles Wilder in his ground-breaking book *New Concepts in Technical Trading Systems.*

Here is a chart of the FTSE 100, with ATR added. It is a great example of high volatility, in this case associated with uncertainty as the market direction changed from down to up, moving to lower volatility, as the new trend up became more established. (You can see my interpretation of this transition in the notes I have put on to the chart.)

ATR – FTSE 100

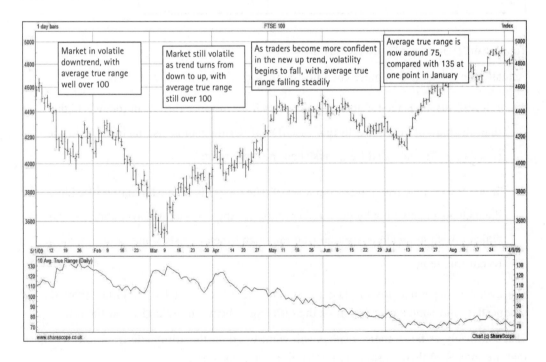

Here is a much simplified example of calculating the average range over the last 10 days of the period covered by this chart.

High	Low	Difference
4859	4737	122
4911	4869	42
4923	4864	59
4927	4872	55
4906	4855	51
4944	4891	53
4921	4820	101
4822	4777	45
4842	4789	53
4874	4828	46
Total:		627

Total of differences = 627, divided by 10 = 63.

Actually the calculation is more complicated than this, for two main reasons:

1. Adjustments are made for gaps. A gap occurs if for instance the low of today is higher than the high of yesterday. In this case the size of the gap is also factored in to the calculation. The adjusted figure is called the "true range".

2. To get the average true range from a set of true ranges is not just a matter of adding them all up and dividing by the number in the set, there is a unique averaging process which takes the previous average true range and then adjusts it based on the most recent true range.

The average true range for the last day in the chart was actually 71, rather than the 63 produced by our simple calculation of the differences between the highs and the lows.

That's probably as far as many readers will want to go on the arithmetic front, but for those that are interested there is some more detail in the Appendix.

Overview of tool

Unlike some tools which measure volatility the concepts behind ATR are fairly easy to understand. In essence, if the range of price movement within each period increases then ATR will increase, if the range of price movement within each period decreases, then ATR will decrease. Over time the volatility of each instrument thus measured will vary.

One benefit of this particular tool is that it provides an objective measure of current volatility for an instrument which can be compared to volatility for the same instrument in other periods. In addition, by dividing the volatility measure by the price of the instrument it is also possible to compare volatility across instruments.

When using ATR we have to decide how many periods to include in the averaging process. Do we want the average of the true range of 5 periods, or of 10 periods or of 14 periods, etc? Most, though not all, trading software packages let the user choose the number of periods.

The strengths of ATR as a volatility measuring tool are:

- simplicity of concept

- objectivity of measurement

- ease of use

- easily programmed and therefore available in most investment/trading software

- applicable on all time frames

- well established and accepted as an analysis tool

A minor weakness of ATR is that because it takes an average over a number of periods, in common with all moving averages it is a lagging indicator. However, this tends not to be a problem in practice, particularly if the user takes care not to select too large a number of periods.

Settings

Partly based on Welles Wilder's book, a commonly used setting for ATR is 14 periods. Other favoured settings include 20 periods, 10 periods and 5 periods. I tend to use a 10 period setting on a daily chart, not only for trades which last from days to weeks but also for day trades. For day trading I like to look at the 10 day ATR, and then use some percentage of it, rather than using for instance the 10 period ATR of a ten minute chart, which is an alternative and perfectly valid approach.

How to use this tool

This tool can help spread bettors as ATR works on two key trading concepts:

1. where to place stops, and

2. how much to bet on a specific trade.

1. Placing stops

There are many techniques to assist stop placement. Here are a selection of places that traders like to put stops:

*   below support if long or above resistance if short

*   below a moving average if long, or above it if short

*   below the low of the last X periods if long, or above the high of the last X periods if short

*   using specialist techniques such as Welles Wilders Parabolic

If using ATR for stop placement, the technique is this:

*   if **long** the stop goes a multiple of ATR *below* a selected point in the last period

*   if **short** the stop goes a multiple of ATR *above* a selected point in the last period

There are two obvious questions to raise here, and one less obvious one.

First of all, which point in the last period should be chosen?

There are at least three options:

1. the **close** of the last period

2. the **high** of the last period (for shorts) or the low of the last period (for longs)

3. the **typical** price of the last period (typical price is calculated as the average of the high the low and the close)

Secondly, what multiple of ATR should be used?

Here there is no simple one-fits-all solution; it will depend on the length of trades being considered, which point in the last period is selected, the type of system, user preferences and the risk profile and objectives of the trader. Here are some options to consider, all based on a 10 day ATR:

- trades expected to last **up to an hour**: 0.1 to 0.2 ATR.

- trades expected to last **up to a day**: 0.2 to 0.5 ATR

- trades expected to last **a few days**: 0.5 to 1.25 ATR

- trades expected to last **a few weeks**: 1.25 to 2.0 ATR

- trades expected to last **several months** at least: 2.0 to 3.5 ATR

Some additional comments need to be made on these options:

1. Stops on trades lasting a few weeks should not be so close to the price that they get hit by normal daily price movement up and down. By definition this daily price movement up and down will average 1 ATR. So for such trades a stop say 1.0 ATR from the close or the typical price is likely to be too close.

2. For a trade lasting a few days the target is usually one move in the right direction with little retracement, so a tight stop (less than 1.0 ATR) can work.

3. When using ATR for stop placement on a day trade it is common to use the entry price as the start point for the calculation.

4. Different ATR figures can be used during the lifetime of a trade; initially quite wide stops can be used, then as the trade comes to its conclusion much closer stops can be used. For instance, on a trade lasting several months the initial stop might be 3.0 ATR from the close, giving the trade room to develop; but then after a large profit has already been obtained the trader might move the stop to say 1.25 ATR away, still allowing the trade to continue if more profit is available, but giving up less profit if the trend reverses.

5. Stop placement should be reviewed on a regular basis – if the trader finds for instance that trades have been getting stopped out too quickly, then a larger ATR multiple should be considered.

6. It is a good idea to use ATR to compare risk to reward – for instance on a trade lasting about a day one might be aiming to capture a 0.5 ATR move with 0.25 ATR risk; or with a trade lasting a few weeks, a 2.5 ATR move with a 1.25 ATR risk. With many successful systems the target reward is at least double the risk.

Thirdly – and this is the less obvious point – the trader has to make a decision whether to move the stop once the trade moves favourably. There are two main techniques here:

1. The initial stop is left at its original spot and if the stop has not been hit the trader picks from a range of exit techniques at the appropriate point in time, for example exiting at a target, exiting at support or resistance, exiting after a certain period of time, to quote just three.

2. The stop is moved during the life of the trade – this is known as a trailing stop. The key technique here is never to move a stop further away from price than it was previously; the stop can only be moved in the direction of the intended trade (i.e up if long, down if short). Each time the stop is moved risk is reduced and, once in profit, more and more of the profit is locked in.

2. Determining bet size

Bet size should be a function of two variables:

1. the distance from the entry point and the initial stop,

2. the percentage of speculative funds the trader wishes to risk on the bet.

We have already seen how the trader can use ATR to determine initial stop placement.

The percentage of speculative funds to be risked on any given bet should be predetermined, taking into account the objectives and risk preferences of the trader, and the profile of the system being used. I have commented in my earlier book, *The Financial Spread Betting Handbook,* on the tendency of spread bettors to risk significantly too high a percentage of their speculative funds on each trade, and this is a common cause of account closure. A well known quote from a US trader suggests that any trader who risks 3% (or more) per trade is "gunslinging".

With these two variables determined, bet size should be calculated automatically. For example:

Variable	Value
Entry	100
Stop	90
Distance from the entry point and the initial stop	10
Speculative funds	£4000
Predetermined risk per spread bet	1% (i.e. £40)
Bet size	£4 per point (£40 divided by 10)

A skilled spread bettor should know this methodology inside out.

Example

We are going to look now at a setup for a short trade in First Group.

ATR charts

Each of the following three charts shows six months of daily price data ending on 10 February 2009. The first chart includes a 5 day ATR, the second chart a 10 day ATR and the third chart a 14 day ATR.

First Group – with 5 Day ATR

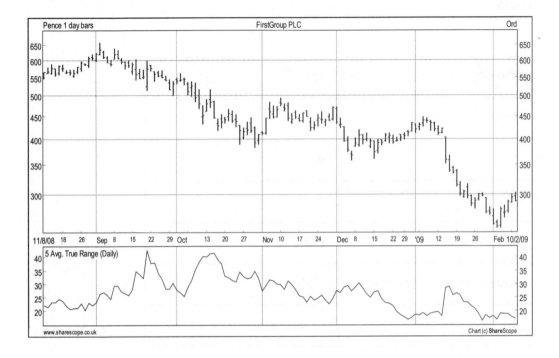

First Group – with 10 Day ATR

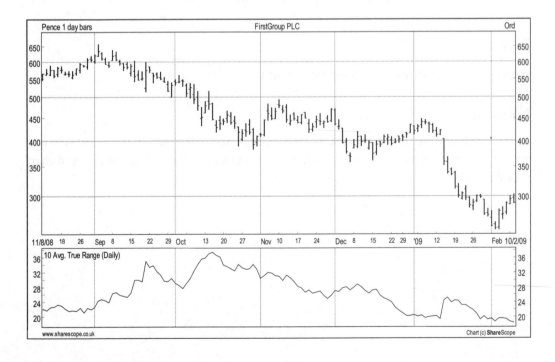

First Group – with 14 Day ATR

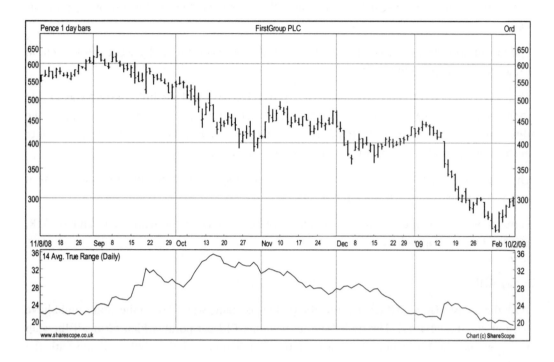

First of all note the difference in range of each ATR indicator across the six months:

- **5 day** ATR range: 16.2 to 42.5

- **10 day** ATR range: 18.3 to 37.5

- **14 day** ATR range: 19.2 to 35.5

The smaller the ATR range the wider the fluctuations in its value since it is more sensitive to daily changes in volatility.

Note however that the three ranges are not very different.

Note finally that across the six months the difference within each range between the lowest and the highest value is wide; with both the 5 and the 10 ATR the highest value is more than double the lowest value, with the 14 day ATR it is not far off double. It makes sense to adjust one's bet size and stop placement to reflect this, so that in times of greatest volatility stops are further away, and bet size is correspondingly smaller.

The trade

Moving on to the short trade, this was a classic pullback setup. Visual inspection shows the stock had been in a powerful downtrend for several months. Over the last five days on the chart the stock had retraced some of that downtrend, with a series of higher highs each day.

At this stage the trader was looking for a sign that the downtrend was reasserting itself, to trigger the short trade. One such trigger was if the stock moved below the low of the previous day.

The low of 10 February 2009 was 288.25, so on this occasion the trader went short when on the next day the price hit 288.0.

This was a short-term trade expected to last just a few days and the initial target was to ride the price down to the most recent low. The trader decided to use an ATR stop, and given the time frame and objectives of the trade selected a stop of 1 ATR from the entry price. The trader decided not to trail the stop until the initial target was hit.

The trader had £20,000 speculative funds dedicated to spread betting and consistently risked 1% of those funds on each trade (i.e. £200).

Let us now see how the 1 ATR stop should have been implemented with each value of ATR, and the impact that had on bet size.

5 day ATR

With the 5 day ATR, 1 ATR (at the time the trade was made) was 17.0, so the stop should have been at 305.0 (288 + 17). The trader should have bet £12 per point, which means if the stop had been hit the loss would have been (305 – 288) times 12 (i.e. £204, in line with the predetermined risk per trade).

10 day ATR

With the 10 day ATR, 1 ATR was 18.3 (price for this stock moved in 0.25p increments, so this was rounded up to 18.5). So the stop should have been at 306.5 (288 + 18.5). The trader should have bet £11 per point, which means if the stop had been hit the loss would have been (306.5 – 288) times 11 (i.e. £203.50), again in line with the predetermined risk per trade.

14 day ATR

With the 14 day ATR, 1 ATR was 19.2, which was rounded up to 19.25. So the stop should have been at 307.25 (288 + 19.25). The trader should have bet £10 per point, which means if the stop had been hit the loss would have been (307.25 – 288) times 10 (i.e. £192.50). Some traders might take a view that they would have been comfortable with £11 per point, giving a loss of £211.75 if the stop was hit. For me personally that would be a little too much over the £200 predetermined risk per trade.

> At some point in the future, the spread betting firms will allow fractions of a pound per point for bets, and then we will be able to risk exactly the amount we want to risk per trade.

Summary of trade calculation for different ATRs

	5 day ATR	10 day ATR	14 day ATR
Trade entry price	288	288	288
ATR (at trade entry)	17.0	18.5	19.25
Stop	305 (208+17)	306.5 (288+18.5)	307.25 (288+19.25)
Bet size (£ per point)	12	11	10
Potential loss (£)	204 (12 x 17)	203.5 (11 x 18.5)	£192.5 (10 x 19.25)

So stop placement and bet size will vary slightly depending on which (period) parameter for ATR is used, but not hugely. I am happy to use the 10 period ATR all the time.

Stop placement – reality check

One final point. One should always do a reality check on where that ATR stop will be. With each ATR value selected above, the stop was above the highest point of the retracement, which was 303p. So that is realistic and consistent with the basic idea behind the trade. If the ATR stop was hit this would also mean that the high of the retracement had been exceeded, which in turn would be a warning sign that perhaps the retracement was not yet over, or even that the downtrend itself was stopping.

For those that want to know the end of the story: the trade was a success, but took longer than originally anticipated. The previous low of the move was hit on the 15th day of the trade, at which point the trader had to make a decision whether to exit the trade, or to move the stop much closer to the latest price.

Alternatives

If you like the idea of ATR, but your software package doesn't have it, here is a simple work around to get a proxy figure. It's not perfect, but workable.

To get a rough equivalent of the 5 period ATR, just calculate the difference between the high and the low for each of the last 5 periods, and average the differences. For the 10 period ATR do a similar calculation for the last 10 periods. You will recall that is exactly what we did earlier in this chapter for the last ten days of the FTSE 100 chart we looked at. If you have spreadsheet facilities on your computer it should be a simple task to build a spreadsheet to do the calculations for you; all you will need to do then is input the highs and the lows for each period.

Conclusion

ATR is:

1. simple and easy to use,

2. can help with stop placement and bet size determination.

1.7900

1.7855

1.7810

TOOL 2:
DIRECTIONAL MOVEMENT

Background and construction

I have already referred to Welles Wilder's book *New Concepts in Technical Trading Systems,* when discussing ATR. Now we look at another concept first described in that historic book, Directional Movement. The main benefit of this tool for traders is that it helps to define whether an instrument is trending or not trending. Since trending markets and non-trending markets usually call for different trading strategies it is clearly useful to be able to determine whether or not a trend is in place.

Let's look at a few months of FTSE 100 price action, with Directional Movement indicators added.

This chart is a great example of the indicator in action. There are three lines on the indicator, and interpretation of the indicator involves all three lines. I have provided a commentary on the indicator action, but particularly note that it is the ADX line that is used to help determine whether the market is trending or not. In this example the chart goes from non-trending action to trending action.

Directional Movement – FTSE 100

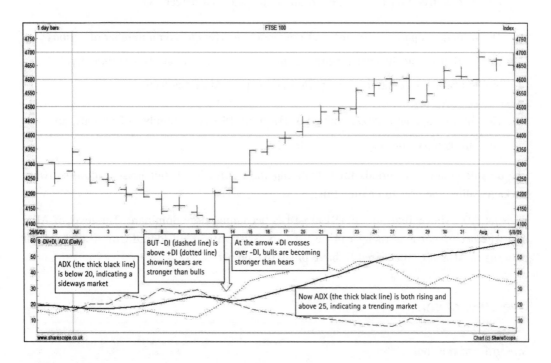

The Directional Movement tool has three components, which in combination can help the trader assess the strength and direction of a trend. We looked in the previous chapter at the concept of "true range". In essence the Directional Movement tool looks at how much of a period's "true range" is outside the "true range" of the previous period.

Here is a simple example using daily figures:

> Today's true range: 100 to 105
>
> Yesterday's true range: 99 to 104
>
> Amount of today's true range that is outside (above in this case) yesterday's true range = 1 (105 – 104)

The actual calculation rules also cover periods which are completely inside the previous period's true range or are both above and below it. (For those who are interested in exploring this further there are more details in the Appendix.)

In an uptrend one would expect on average part of a period's range to be above the previous period's range; in a downtrend, on average part of a period's range to be below the previous period's range.

1.   The first component, **+DI**, looks at how much on average over a number of periods each period's range has exceeded the previous period's range. This is then divided by the average true range of the period and expressed as a percentage.

2.   The second component, **–DI**, looks at how much on average over a number of periods each period's range has been below the previous period's range. This is then divided by the average true range of the period and expressed as a percentage.

3.   The third component, **ADX**, compares +DI and –DI over a number of periods, and puts this comparison on a scale of 0 to 100.

The default number of periods for calculating the figures is 14, but most trading software packages allow the user to change this.

A rising ADX shows that one of +DI or –DI is becoming more dominant. The level of ADX and whether or not it is rising can be used to assist with trend identification; and certain patterns in ADX are considered to have predictive power.

Overview of tool

Strengths of the tool

The strengths of Directional Movement as a trend measuring tool are:

*   provides an objective measure

- can be used as a filter to switch from trend following to counter-trend methods and vice versa

- easily programmed and therefore available in many trading software programs

- applicable on all time frames

- well established and accepted as an analysis tool, particularly in the US

Weaknesses of the tool

The weaknesses of Directional Movement are:

- although the basic building blocks of the tool are quite straightforward the way it is assembled is quite complex and the total package takes a little getting used to

- although the actual calculations of the three components are objective the interpretation of the interplay of the three components does often require some interpretation

- containing as they do moving average calculations the three components do lag price action; there are times when the tool indicates a trend, but the trend is over, particularly after a fast move in one direction followed by a fast reversal (a "spike"). Equally there are times when a trend is obvious to visual inspection but the tool has yet to record the fact.

On balance, however, users of this tool will maintain that these weaknesses are minor compared with the huge potential benefits available to the trader experienced in interpretation of the tool.

Settings

The standard setting for the three components of the Directional Movement tool, +DI, -DI and ADX, is 14 periods. This was the setting used by Welles Wilder when he first introduced the tool. A number of other settings have been used successfully by traders over the years, including 8, 10, 13 and 18.

The website www.spreadbettingcentral.co.uk uses two settings, the standard 14 period setting (on a daily chart), and a faster 8 period setting. Analysis of the seven instruments tracked regularly on that site takes into account both settings.

Other analysts, for example Dr Schaap, like to use one setting for +DI and –DI and another for ADX.

How to use this tool

In an uptrend +DI will rise above –DI, as on average the range of each period which is outside the previous period's range will tend to be on the upside. Conversely, in a downtrend –DI will rise above +DI, as on average the range of each period which is outside the previous period's range will tend to be on the downside. In a trading range the +DI and –DI lines will often cross over each other repeatedly.

The first check with this indicator is to see which of +DI and –DI is higher. Generally if +DI is above –DI one will not be searching for opportunities to go short, and if –DI is above +DI one will not be searching for opportunities to go long.

But the real value of this tool lies in the ADX component.

There are two main schools of thought on interpreting ADX; one looks at the level of ADX, the other at whether it is rising or not. My personal preference is to look at both. There are a number of specific ADX patterns which are considered to have predictive power. Overall, ADX is most effective when combined with other analysis techniques.

Level of ADX

Many traders, particularly in the US, use an ADX level of 30 as a cut-off point. Above 30 is considered to represent a trend, below 30 is not. Others use 25 as that cut-off point. Others still use 20.

Having a cut-off point may well assist in filtering a large range of instruments. For instance if your trading universe encompasses 5000+ US stocks, and you are looking for established trends, then a computerised search for all stocks with an ADX level above say 25 might be the first step in building a shortlist.

ADX rising

Others prefer to look at whether ADX is rising or not. The thinking here is that if ADX is rising this means one or other of +DI and –DI is becoming more powerful, which in turn means there is increasing momentum either up or down – what one would expect as a trend gathers pace. By contrast a declining ADX signifies loss of momentum either up or down. In a trend, this could just represent a temporary loss of momentum during a pullback, alternatively it might be the beginning of the end of the trend.

Level of a rising ADX

My preference when using ADX to identify potential trading candidates is to look for a rising ADX above a certain cut-off level.

There are trade-offs in selecting the cut-off level.

- A **low level**, such as 15, will provide a higher number of trading candidates, and it will be possible to catch some powerful trends near their beginning. However at the 15 level there will also be many instruments which never fully develop a trend. Potentially there will be more losers, but it gives the potential to capture a higher percentage of a trend when it does fully develop, and therefore potentially some large winners.

- A **higher level** of cut off for a rising ADX, such as 25, will produce a lower number of trading candidates, and potentially less candidates that never develop a full trend. However, trends will tend to be entered later. This for many will not be an issue, because for many the whole point of the type of trading undertaken by spread bettors is to find a well established trend, join it for a while, exit, and go in search of another trend; as opposed to capturing large chunks of one trend.

I use different levels of a rising ADX at different times.

For example, when the overall stock market is in a powerful up or downtrend I will be keener to use trend following strategies on individual stocks, and might select a cut-off point of 20 for the rising ADX as one of my selection criteria. In a sideways market, or where I am already close to a predetermined maximum limit for the number of open trades I hold, I might raise the cut off to 30.

The ADX setting will also affect the number of potential trading candidates. If for instance one decides to go looking for instruments with a rising ADX over 20, if an 8 day ADX is used this will generate many more trading candidates than if a 14 day ADX is used, because it takes longer for the 14 day ADX to rise. But the same trade-offs apply as when we looked at using a lower cut-off point for the rising ADX, more trading candidates does not necessarily mean more overall success.

More often than not the criteria I use for defining a trend using this tool are:

1. 8 period ADX 25 or above, *and*

2. 14 period ADX 20 or above, *and*

3. 14 period ADX flat or rising.

Specific ADX patterns

There are a number of specific ADX patterns which traders use. I mention here three of the best known of these:

1. ADX turn down

2. ADX turn up

3. DI crossovers

1. ADX turn down

This is mentioned in the original Welles Wilder text, and is well worth paying attention to – not so much as an entry signal but as a warning to exit an existing position at least partially or to tighten stops.

The signal occurs when during a trend ADX rises above both DI lines, and then turns down. This often leads to a halt in the trend or to a retracement; this may be a temporary phenomenon, after which the trend reasserts itself, or it can represent a significant turning point. Either way the reward-to-risk profile of the trade may well have changed, and at the very least this calls for a detailed assessment of the trade.

One possibility following this signal is to take profits on a portion of the trade and move the stop much closer on the balance. This signal can be useful to the trader when using a 14 period setting. The 8 period setting produces more frequent turn downs, and the signal is less effective with the faster setting.

2. ADX turn up

This is a technique referred to in Dr Alexander Elder's classic book *Trading for a Living* as the single best signal that this tool produces, one which can capture the birth of a new trend.

The signal occurs when ADX falls and then stays below both DI lines (the longer it stays the more powerful the base for the next move) and then rises by at least 4 from its lowest point below both DI lines. If +DI is then higher than –DI this signals a potential long trade, if –DI is higher than +DI this signals a potential short trade.

3. DI crossovers

Back to the original Welles Wilder text once more. When one DI line crosses up over another this creates the potential for a new trade. For the new trade to be triggered though a further step is required: if +DI has crossed up over –DI, then in addition price must rise above the high of the day that the crossover occurred; if –DI has crossed up over +DI, then in addition price must drop below the low of the day that the crossover occurred.

Combining ADX with other techniques

It is common for ambitious traders to go in search of the perfect indicator, one which will solve all their trading problems. I am doubtful that any such indicator exists. Powerful though ADX is as a tool, it should always be combined with other techniques.

For example, we look later at support and resistance. If ADX tells me there is a strong downtrend, but I identify that price has persistently turned round at a price level close to the current price I will probably want to delay going short on the instrument until it shows signs of being able to get below that support level.

We also look at moving averages later, and some traders that use ADX will also want their chosen moving averages to be consistent with the ADX message before making a trading decision.

Finally, it is often important to confirm any ADX message via visual inspection. Even if ADX suggests a trend is in place, many traders will not make a trading decision based on it unless the trend is also apparent via visual inspection of the chart.

Example

In the remaining charts in this chapter I will use my most frequent criteria for trend identification as described earlier which (just to remind ourselves) is this:

1.   8 period ADX 25 or above, *and*

2.   14 period ADX 20 or above, *and*

3.   14 period ADX flat or rising.

In an uptrend +DI is above –DI. In a downtrend –DI is above +DI.

On both the 8 day and the 14 day ADX charts the following legend applies:

• ADX is shown by the thick black line

• +DI is shown by the dotted line

• -DI is shown by the dashed line

We will look at three charts, an uptrend, a sideways trend and a downtrend.

Uptrend

The first chart is of the ETF Lyxor Gold Bullion Securities Ltd, which tracks the price of gold (multiply by 10 to get the gold price) – and is an easy way therefore to monitor gold prices.

It will be used in this example to trigger a spread bet on the gold price itself.

Lyxor Gold Bullion Securities

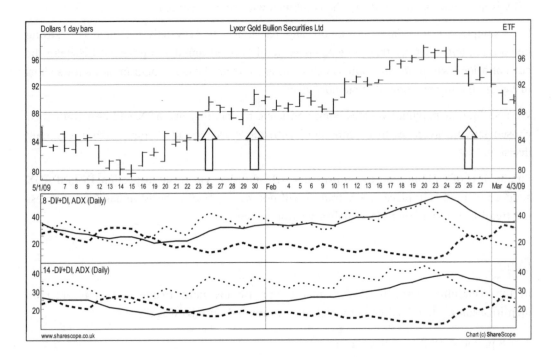

There are three arrows drawn on this chart.

1. At the **first arrow**, for the first time on this chart the 14 period ADX reached 20, and was rising, while the 8 period ADX had already reached 25. This instrument therefore came on our radar at this point since it now met our criteria for a trend. Note that in addition to visual inspection we know it is an uptrend rather than a downtrend because +DI is above –DI.

2. At the **second arrow** for the three previous days price has been retracing the uptrend, giving us a potential opportunity to join the trend on a pullback. On the day the arrow points to, price exceeded the high of the previous day, giving us our signal during the day to enter. This in fact happened at the open the next day, and the entry price in gold itself would have been around $891. Suppose a 1 ATR stop (per the last chapter) had been set. The 10 day ATR (not shown) in the ETF stood at 2.36, equivalent to $23.6 in the price of gold itself. Let us assume this time that the trader

had £25,000 of speculative funds. Even with this amount in the spread betting account the trader could only afford £1 per point of gold, since gold bets are priced in pounds per $0.1; so with a stop $23.6 away this represents £236 of risk, just under 1%.

3. The **third arrow** represents the point at which the 14 day ADX indicator gave a warning sign – it turned down from above the +DI and the –DI lines, representing a slowing down in the trend leading either to a retracement or even to the end of the trend. In this case this was a signal for the trader to exit this trade the next day. An exit at the open the next day would have been at around $926. Total movement between entry and exit was $35, which at £1 per point would have been a profit of £350, versus a risk of £236 (not spectacular).

Sideways trend

Following a steep downtrend in the second half of 2008, the currency pair Sterling Dollar (GBPUSD) moved into a sideways trend for several months. Here is a chart showing that sideways trend, and it shows clearly how ADX behaves in a sideways market.

Sterling Dollar

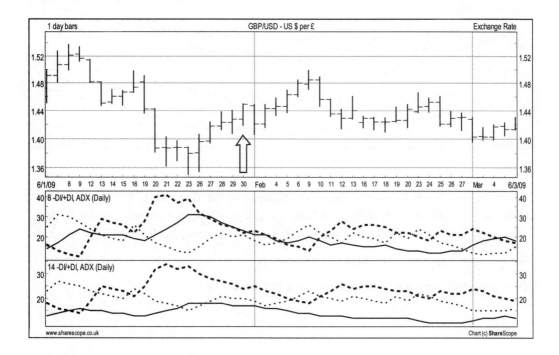

Look at the period after the arrow. The day of the arrow was the day when the 8 day ADX dropped below 25. During the sideways market which followed both the 8 day and the 14 day ADX levels remained at low levels, signifying a lack of a trend and indicating that this was a market unsuitable for trend following strategies. At one point the 8 day ADX falls to as low as 12, and the 14 day ADX falls to as low as 10. Typical for this type of market the ADX line is frequently below both of the DI lines, and the two DI lines crisscross each other.

Downtrend

After a period of sideways movement the stock Compass Group PLC developed a downtrend in early February 2009.

Compass Group

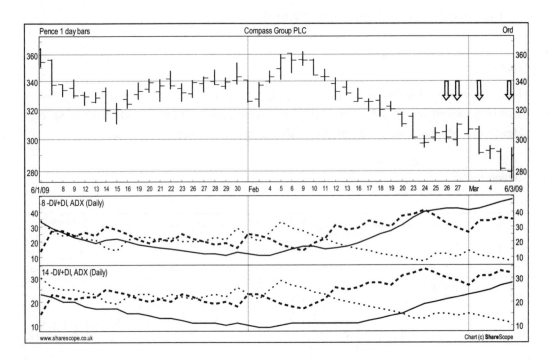

First of all note the behaviour of the ADX indicator in the first half of the chart, which is similar to the chart of Sterling Dollar which we have just looked – sideways action in price, matched by low levels of ADX and the two DI lines crisscrossing each other.

Now see what happens to the ADX and DI lines as the downtrend starts in early February.

–DI crosses decisively over +DI, and the ADX line begins to rise.

The **first arrow** on the chart marks the point when the 14 day ADX first gets to the 20 level (21 to be precise), at which time the 8 day ADX is already as high as 41. At this point the stock comes on to our radar as a potential down bet. The remaining three arrows show the setup for and implementation of a trade in this stock.

At the **second arrow** there had now been a retracement of the downtrend for three days, with a higher high each day. We decide to go short if price falls below the low of this third day of retracement. However, this does not occur on the following day, and there is a fourth day of retracement. Now we decide to go short if price falls below the low of this fourth day of retracement.

The **third arrow** shows that the following day price did indeed fall below the low of the fourth day of retracement, and we went short at 302.75p. Suppose we were of the opinion that the market overall had fallen a lot in a short space of time; we might have decided to just play this for a quick profit. 1 ATR in this stock (not shown) was 12.5p. Let us say we decided to have a stop 12.5p away, and to exit as soon as we have a profit of twice our initial risk, i.e. 25p profit. Entry at 302.75p, stop at 315.25p, profit target at 277.75p.

The **fourth arrow** shows when that profit target was reached.

For busy people with little time during the day this trade could have been automated. On the day of entry a stop order to enter could have been placed at 302.75p with a contingent order to buy at 315.25. Once in the trade the contingent order could have been cancelled and replaced with an OCO order (One Cancels the Other) – a stop order to buy at 315.25p and a limit order to buy at 277.75p; whichever order gets filled first the other one gets cancelled.

Alternatives

An alternative and more recent tool used by some analysts to help identify when an instrument moves from trending to not trending, and vice versa, is the *Aroon indicator*, developed by Tushar Chande. The building blocks for the Aroon indicator are two calculations: the number of periods since a recent high within a user-defined period, and the number of periods within that user-defined period since a recent low. These are used to generate two lines, Aroon Up and Aroon Down, and interpretation of the indicator is based on the interplay between these two lines.

Conclusion

It is clearly important to the trader to know when an instrument is trending and when it is not. ADX is a very useful tool which can help with that analysis, particularly if combined with other tools such as visual inspection.

1.7900

1.7855

1.7810

TOOL 3: MOVING AVERAGES

Background and construction

Moving averages have been used by analysts for many years. There are several different types of moving average that are popular with traders, and many different combinations of periods used to create them, but the principles of how to use them are much the same whichever type is used. Moving averages can be used in all timescales.

Let's look at a weekly chart of the FTSE 100 with a 4 period, a 10 period and a 40 period simple moving average on it. I have included commentary on the chart, showing how the combination of the averages moves from downtrend mode to sideways mode to uptrend mode.

Moving averages – FTSE 100

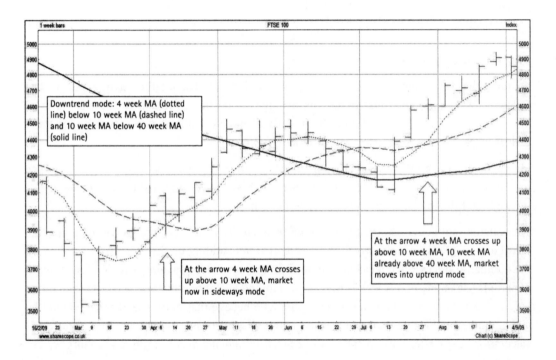

Moving averages, as the name suggests, take an average of a series of prices and then update that average each time a new price occurs.

Here is a how the 4 period simple moving average is calculated using the close of 4 consecutive weeks on the FTSE 100 chart.

End of week	Close
14/08/09	4714
21/08/09	4851
28/08/09	4909
04/09/09	4852
Total	19,326

19,326 divided by 4 = 4832

So the 4 week moving average on 4/09/09 would be plotted on the chart as 4832. The following week (on 11/09/09) the moving average would be re-calculated: the closing price on 14/08/09 would be dropped, and the moving average calculated as the average for the 4 end-of-week closing prices from 21/08/09 to 11/09/09.

Moving averages can be calculated on any series of price data, not just on closes. For instance on highs, on lows, or on combinations of these such as *typical price* (which is the average of the high and the low and the close for each period).

The calculation above describes a *simple moving average* – where every price in the calculation is given an equal weight by virtue of simply adding up the prices and dividing by the number of prices. Such a calculation may be fine for moving averages with a low number of periods (e.g. 4 day or 4 week). However, for moving averages that cover a longer time range (e.g. 200 day, 50 week), there are some people who believe that more recent prices should be given more weight than prices from, say, a year previously. To answer this a different calculation is sometimes used: called an *exponential moving average*, this gives more weight to more recent prices.

There are other types of moving average, but most traders use either simple or exponential. (The other types are briefly described in an appendix.)

Here is another chart of the FTSE 100 with annotation showing how an exponential moving average follows the price action more closely.

Exponential moving average – FTSE 100

Overview of tool

One of the benefits of moving averages is that they help the trader see the wood for the trees – what some might regard as random short-term price movements around a longer-term movement (up, down or sideways) are partially eliminated. A jagged line which would be created by joining up the individual prices turns into a smoother line when a line is created joining up the average prices.

Moving averages can be used to create trading signals. For instance, crossovers of moving averages, either price crossing the moving average, or one moving average crossing another, or crossing involving multiple moving averages, have a long history of use in the design of mechanical trading systems. These signals tend to work well in trending markets but lose money in sideways markets.

Moving averages can also be used to assist with trend identification, and this will be our primary focus of attention in this chapter. Simply put, in an uptrend the moving average will point upwards, in a downtrend it will point downwards, and in a sideways market it will point sideways.

The importance of timescale

It sometimes surprises traders than an instrument can simultaneously be in an uptrend, a downtrend and a sideways market. But this just depends what timescale is being considered.

Take the old and familiar example of the 20, 50 and 200 day moving averages used by investors in analysis of stocks:

- the **200 day** moving average (representative of the long-term trend) can be pointing up, signifying an *uptrend*;

- the **50 day** moving average (representative of the intermediate term) can be flat, representing a *sideways market*; and

- the **20 day** moving average, representative of the short term (for an investor) can be pointing down, signifying a *downtrend*.

In fact in some circumstances this combination of moving averages might offer a potential opportunity to go long the instrument.

Strengths of moving averages

The strengths of moving averages as a trend identification tool are:

- provides an objective measure,

- conceptually straightforward and easy to use,

- easily programmed and therefore available in probably every investment/trading software program,

- applicable on all time frames, and

- long pedigree.

Weaknesses of moving averages

The weaknesses of moving averages as a trend identification tool are:

- moving averages lag the price action, the longer the time frame the more they lag, so when used as part of an exit methodology their signals can be late,

- on any one instrument different moving averages seem to work better than others at different times, and so trading systems using moving averages can back-test well with a particular combination of moving averages over one period, and then do dismally over another; this problem can be partly overcome by using this tool in combination with other tools (such as ADX).

Settings

There are almost as many settings for moving averages as there are traders. The decisions required are:

1. which type of moving average to use,

2. which price data to apply the moving average to,

3. how many moving averages to use, and

4. what number of periods to use for each moving average.

Here is just one group of settings for trading using spread bets that last a few days to a few weeks:

- A 20 day simple moving average just for use in a standard setting for Bollinger bands (not covered in this book) – I strongly recommend John Bollinger's book, aptly named *Bollinger on Bollinger Bands* (McGraw-Hill, 2002).

- A 4 day, a 9 day and an 18 day exponential moving average of typical price (high plus low plus close, divided by three). This particular combination of three moving averages has a long pedigree, although it is usually applied to closing prices.

How to use this tool

The moving averages are used to assist with trend identification in two main ways:

1. the **order** of the moving averages, and

2. the **slope** of the moving averages.

1. Order

For an uptrend to be identified the shortest moving average must be above the middle moving average and the middle one must be above the longest: with the 4-9-18 combination therefore, 4 must be above 9 and 9 must be above 18.

For a downtrend to be diagnosed the shortest moving average must be below the middle moving average and the middle one must be below the longest: with the 4-9–18 combination therefore, 4 must be below 9 and 9 must be below 18.

Any other alignment is diagnosed as a sideways market.

It is worth thinking briefly about what happens during a transition from one type of market to another; this will clarify the logic of why the order of the moving averages is important.

Let's consider the case of a sideways market moving into an uptrend. In a perfect sideways market price won't move at all, so all three averages will be static (flat) and on top of each other (having the same value). As the market moves into an uptrend the first moving average to change position will be the shortest one, which stays closest to prices, and on which each day's change makes a more immediate impact. So the shortest one will rise above the other two. Next to move up will be the middle moving average, but now the shortest one will have moved more up, so now the moving averages will have moved into the uptrend configuration described above.

2. Slope

For many analysts the slope of a moving average is its most important feature. In a strong uptrend all three moving averages will be rising (pointing up). With well chosen moving averages, during retracements/pullbacks in the trend the longest moving average will continue to point up, but the middle moving average may begin to flatten or even turn down slightly and the shortest moving average will often turn down. These pullbacks often provide good opportunities to enter the trend.

In a strong downtrend all three moving averages will be falling (pointing down). During retracements the longest moving average should continue to point down, the middle one may flatten or even begin to turn up and the shortest one will often turn up. Again, these retracements often provide good opportunities to enter the trend.

Example

In this section we will be using a combination of three exponential moving averages, 4, 9 and 18, based on the daily typical price (high plus low plus close, divided by three). These three moving averages are shown on the charts in the following way:

- 4 day moving average – dotted line

- 9 day moving average – dashed line

- 18 day moving average – solid line

Since we are using moving averages to assist with trend identification, and ADX was also used to assist with trend identification, we will revisit each of the instruments we looked at in the ADX chapter to see if we get the same message from our chosen moving average combination.

Uptrend

Here is the instrument we used to look at an uptrend in the ADX chapter.

Lyxor Gold Bullion Securities

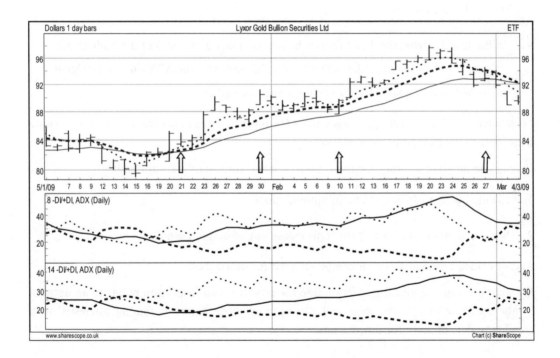

Let us see what happened on the chart at each of the four arrows drawn on it:

- At the **first arrow** the moving averages have now moved into uptrend mode – the 4 day is above the 9 day and the 9 day is above the 18 day; all three are rising. Note that this tool produces earlier notification of an uptrend than the ADX tool: this tool flags it up on 21 January, the ADX tool flagged it up on 26 January. But remember the trade-off rule: earlier signals are usually coupled with a higher percentage of false signals.

- The **second arrow** is where we took the trade in the previous chapter, following the three day retracement, and exactly the same logic would have led to a trade here using the moving average tool instead of the ADX tool.

- At the **third arrow** some minor retracements have caused the fastest moving average, the 4 day, to begin to turn down. This is a common situation; the 4 day might turn down and the 9 day might go flat or even turn down; and the 18 day might go flat. This does not signify the end of the trend, and in some situations may represent a low risk opportunity to enter the trend. Note that by the time the 18 day average turns down, usually the 4 day will have crossed down below the 9 day, which using this tool is a signal to exit.

- At the **fourth arrow** the 4 day crosses below the 9 day and if still in the trade that is a signal to exit at the open the next morning; interestingly the ADX turn down signal we looked at in the last chapter occurred one day earlier.

Traders who use both moving averages and ADX together have to decide whether they require both tools to be giving the same message.

Here is one possible solution for those traders, when considering an uptrend:

1. to enter, both tools have to be in uptrend mode,

2. but exit as soon as either of the tools comes out of uptrend mode.

And of course a similar solution can be adopted for downtrends.

My solution is to add visual inspection into the mix. If visual inspection points to an uptrend I only need one of the two tools to be in uptrend mode before becoming interested in a possible trade; similarly for downtrends.

Sideways market

Here is the instrument we used to look at a sideways market in the ADX chapter.

Sterling Dollar

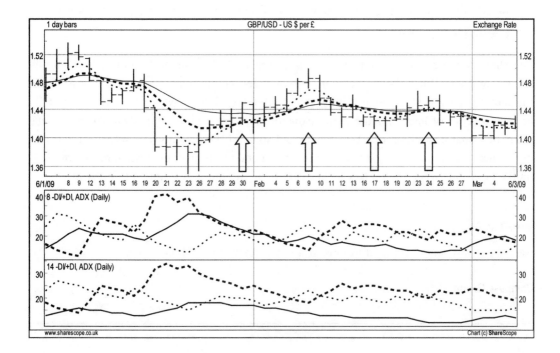

There are four arrows on this chart:

- At the **first arrow** the moving averages, having previously been in downtrend mode (with the 4 day below the 9 day and the 9 day below the 18 day), now move into sideways mode (the 4 day has crossed back up over the 9 day). If the trader was short this was a warning to exit the trade. This move into sideways mode actually coincided with the 8 day ADX moving below 25 – this will not always be the case.

- At the **second arrow** the moving averages have gone into uptrend mode (4 above 9 and 9 above 18); this signal was precipitate and any trader going long at this point would have lost money. Applying the three criteria of visual inspection, ADX and moving averages, since only one of them was indicating an uptrend this instrument was not on my personal short-list for long trades at this point.

- At the **third arrow** the moving averages have moved into downtrend mode (4 below 9 and 9 below 18), though once again neither ADX nor visual inspection suggests a downtrend.

- At the **fourth arrow** anyone who had gone short the instrument received a warning to exit since the moving averages had moved into sideways mode again (the 4 day crossing up over the 9 day).

This shows quite clearly the dangers of using three fairly fast moving averages without any additional filters. When the market is in quite a wide trading range it is perfectly possible for the moving averages to move briefly into uptrend or into downtrend mode, potentially causing a series of losses for the trader (sometimes referred to as whipsaws). The additional filters of visual inspection and ADX help avoid some of these whipsaws; however the trade-off of these additional filters is that a number of good trades may be missed, or entered late, on the occasions when the market moves convincingly into a new uptrend or downtrend.

Downtrend

Here is the instrument we used to look at a downtrend in the ADX chapter.

Compass Group

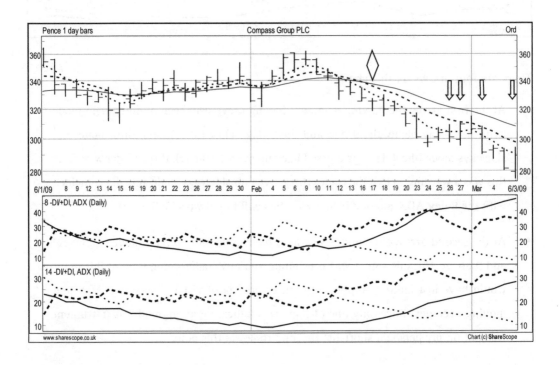

The arrows on this chart have been left exactly as they were in the ADX chapter. The second third and fourth arrows are as before:

- **Second arrow** – there is a setup for a potential long trade based on a three day pullback in the trend.

- **Third arrow** – the day of entry, as price fell below the previous day's low.

- **Fourth arrow** – the day of exit, based on a target of two times the initial risk.

What is interesting is the difference between the diamond drawn on the chart and the first arrow.

Remember, the first arrow shows when ADX went into uptrend mode. The diamond shows when the moving average combination moved from sideways mode to downtrend mode (4 below 9 and 9 below 18). Here is that trade-off we discussed above. Whereas the ADX filter stopped us getting a run of whipsaws when the market went sideways, here waiting for ADX to move into uptrend mode means we have waited seven trading days since the moving averages went into uptrend mode. The good news in this particular case is that if we trade on pullbacks it made no difference, we didn't miss any pullback trades in those seven days. In this case, also, the downtrend was a lot clearer to visual inspection than when the moving averages first moved into downtrend mode.

Alternatives

If your trading software does not let you create a moving average of typical price, then the most obvious alternative is to use closing prices.

If you like the concept of using three moving averages together there are of course many other combinations possible. One US author advocates 10, 20 and 30, another 14, 30 and 50. A traditional longer-term combination for stock market investors is 20, 50 and 200. In principle the longer the moving average the more it will smooth the price action but also the more it will lag behind it. The longer moving averages tend to be of more interest to those with a longer time frame for trading.

Conclusion

Many uses have been found for this tool over the years, but the technique of using it to assist with trend identification is simple and powerful.

1.7900

1.7855

1.7810

TOOL 4:
SUPPORT AND RESISTANCE

Background and construction

Support and resistance in simple terms is shorthand for price levels where moves down or moves up have stopped in the past. The idea is not new. A hundred years ago books referred to such levels, even if they didn't use the words support and resistance. The basic assumption the trader makes when placing trades using these levels is that if these levels have stopped price moves in the past they will do so again; and if they don't the signal to exit should be clear.

Let's look at a chart of the FTSE 100 from mid-2009. The chart shows an area of resistance and an area of support, which represent key areas in the continual struggle between the bulls and the bears.

Support and resistance – FTSE 100

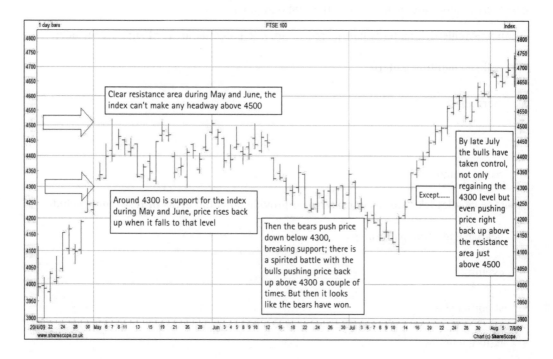

There are many different ways to identify support and resistance levels, ranging from very simple to quite complex. Complex is not necessarily better.

Simple

At the simplest level we have visual inspection of a chart to identify clear levels where price has in the past stopped going up or stopped going down. Particularly when price has been in a defined range for an extended period of time, support and resistance levels are very clear visually. The price action can seem to fall within a neat geometric pattern such as a rectangle, and a strategy of selling when price reaches the top of the rectangle and buying when it reaches the bottom of the rectangle can be very effective until price eventually breaks out of the rectangle.

More complex

At a more complex level we have specific patterns which are considered by some analysts to have predictive value. For instance there are a whole host of 1, 2 and 3 bar patterns that can be diagnosed using Japanese candlestick charts and which are considered to provide potential areas of support or resistance. A number of recent books that have carried out detailed testing on these patterns have called into question how reliable some of these patterns actually are, but there are nonetheless a large number of traders who use them successfully. (This is not a book about Japanese candlesticks, but for those interested in doing more research some of the best known books are mentioned in the bibliography.)

Japanese candlestick patterns considered to provide potential areas of support include:

- bullish engulfing pattern

- morning star

- hammer

- rising window

Japanese candlestick patterns considered to provide potential areas of resistance include:

- bearish engulfing pattern

- evening star

- shooting star

- falling window

Additional uses of the support and resistance concept

The concept of support and resistance is also expanded by some analysts to incorporate non-horizontal levels. The most common uses here are:

- *Trend lines*
  A rising line is drawn beneath rising prices, and this line is extended into the future to predict possible areas where falls in prices may be halted; a falling line is drawn above

falling prices, and this line is extended into the future to predict possible areas where rises in prices may be halted.

- *Moving averages*
  Some analysts use moving averages in the same way as trend lines, as a kind of curvilinear trend line, to predict possible areas where falls or rises in prices may be halted in the future. They might refer for instance to "support" offered by the 50 day moving average.

- *Fibonacci levels*
  Some analysts use Fibonacci retracement levels to predict possible areas where falls or rises in prices may be halted in the future; aficionados place special emphasis on certain retracements such 38.2%, 50% and 61.8% (all three based on the mathematical concept of the Fibonacci series of numbers).

Overview of tool

The tool is fairly simple to understand. Taking support first; support is a level where price has fallen to in the past and then stopped falling. Once a *support level* has been identified, if price approaches that level again a low risk trade can be entered with a stop below the support level, anticipating a move up away from the support level.

Correspondingly, resistance is a level where price has risen to in the past and then stopped rising. Once a *resistance level* has been identified, if price approaches that level again a low risk trade can be entered with a stop above the resistance level, anticipating a move down away from the resistance level.

Strengths of support and resistance

The strengths of the tool are:

- conceptually straightforward

- applicable on all time frames

- long pedigree

Weaknesses of support and resistance

The weaknesses of the tool are:

- Identification of support and resistance levels has not to date been automated, and in some cases may require some subjective input from the analyst. So although the concept is simple, practical implementation may not be so simple.

- Support and resistance levels do fail, and when they do there can be powerful moves down through support or up through resistance; trading with them does sometimes therefore require quick reactions, or preferably automated stops, to protect potential losses to trading capital.

Settings

This tool is not an indicator with a scale of value and does not have settings as such. There are however some traditional yardsticks for assessing the strength of support or resistance. These are largely common sense:

- the number of times price has visited a level of support or resistance (the more the better);

- the number of periods the support or resistance level has been in evidence (the longer the better); and

- the volume (total value of transactions) there has been when price has turned around (the more the better).

I would add another: the more obvious the support or resistance level the better. If everyone sees a support or resistance level and expects everyone else to be trading off it the whole thing can become a self-fulfilling prophecy.

There is also a key feature of support and resistance, sometimes referred to as the polarity principle: support once broken tends to become resistance, resistance once broken tends to become support.

My preferred technique

My preferred technique for identifying support and resistance areas is to identify (on multiple time frames) a specific pattern sometimes referred to as a fractal. On a daily chart, for an area of support I am looking for three bars where the middle bar has a lower low than the two outer bars.

Why?

Because that low point in the middle bar represents a point where in one battle in the ongoing battle between the bulls and the bears a significant event took place. The bears pushed price down as far as they could, to that point, but at that point the bulls retook control and buyers came into the market to lift prices. If I can find one such fractal that is worth noting, if there are two at the same level that is even more important, since that means that at this point the bears have now lost their grip on proceedings twice.

I mentioned multiple time frames. I always like to move at least one time frame up to look for fractals there too. If I am trading mainly off daily charts I like to know how the land lies on the weekly chart too.

A support area based on a weekly fractal is based on the same principle: the low point in the middle bar is where the bears on that occasion lost their grip on proceedings, but over a three week period rather than just a three day period, and therefore even more significant.

If I can find more than one fractal on the weekly chart, backed up a number of fractals in a similar area on the daily chart I will have some confidence that this level will offer potential support.

The principles for identifying resistance levels are exactly the same, except the other way up. The fractal now should be three bars with the middle bar having a higher high than the two outer bars. This is the point to which the bulls could lift prices, but no further, then the bears took control; a significant event.

Three additional points here:

1. Don't expect these support and resistance levels to be so neat and orderly that they are all at exactly the same price; more often support and resistance levels are represented by a small range of prices rather than just one.

2. The reason why this tool works is that traders remember or recognise on a chart that this is where price turned around before; support and resistance that developed beyond the memory of most traders can tend to be less effective. There are no clear rules of thumb here, but as an example if I am trading primarily off a daily chart expecting a trade to last a month I would be really interested in any fractals I could find going back three months. I might take note of obvious ones even going back eighteen months, but I would not be looking for any say four years back. If I was mapping out the big picture using a weekly chart of an index I would be very interested in fractals over the last year, I might take note of obvious ones going back five years, and on occasion I might go back much further. There are traders and

investors who will be aware for instance what the low of the last bear market was, or the high of the last bull market, and might make trading decisions if those points are reached again.

3. Don't expect price to turn around bang on an identified support or resistance level; the levels are not like a solid floor or ceiling which will hold price up or stop it rising; price can often go marginally through a support or resistance level before turning round.

How to use this tool

There are three main ways to use this tool:

1. trading strategies can be built just around buying support and selling resistance,

2. when entering a trend, support and resistance can be used to identify low risk entry points, and

3. when in a trade support and resistance levels can be used to assist with setting initial and trailing stops.

Each of these is illustrated in the charts below.

Example

We look in this section at how support and resistance can be used in various types of markets. In sideways markets we are potentially interested in both long and short trades, but our first example looks at buying support. In trending markets we can use support and resistance both to identify low risk entry points to the trend and to assist with stop placement. In principle we will be looking to take trades in line with the trend, so in an uptrend we will be looking to buy support and in a downtrend we will be looking to sell resistance, rather than the other way round. We look at both an uptrend and a downtrend to illustrate these points.

Sideways market

Here is a chart of the stock Antofagasta.

Antofagasta

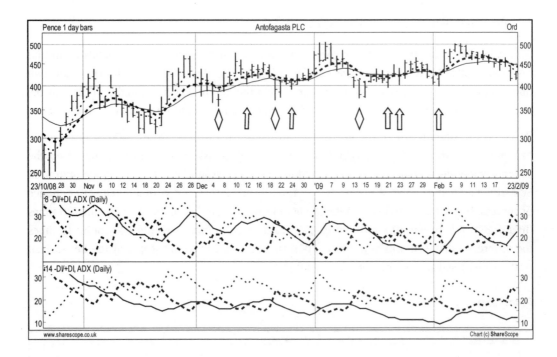

From early to December to the far right of the chart (23 February 2009) the instrument was in sideways mode. There are three separate indications of this:

1. the sideways market is clear to **visual inspection,**

2. apart from a two day period when the 14 day **ADX** rose to 20, for the rest of the time it was in sideways mode below 20, and

3. the **moving averages** crisscross each other, swinging from uptrend to downtrend mode, producing whipsaws.

In a sideways market it is possible to go long or short if clear support or resistance levels can be found and the reward-to-risk ratio looks favourable.

In this case there are clear support levels.

Each arrow and each diamond on the chart shows fractals where the middle bar has a lower low than either of the two bars on either side of it. As mentioned before, this marks the battleground where on a previous occasion the bulls managed to stop price falling and turned things around. The arrows are at approximately one level, and the diamonds at another. The actual values of the low points in each of the fractals are:

- arrows, left to right, 402.25, 389.75, 393.5, 399.75, 397.25

- diamonds, left to right, 355.25, 367.75, 371.0

If a trade were taken it is clear that there is some resistance in the form of fractals at around just above 500. Make sure you are comfortable locating them for yourself. There are two obvious ones, you are looking for three bars where the middle bar has a higher high than the two outer ones. There are two different trades that could be structured around buying support.

Based on the support where the arrows are one might try to buy around 400 to get a move to around 500 with a stop at say 390, a great reward to risk ratio of 10 to 1. Based on the support where the diamonds are one could look to buy at around 400 to get a move to around 500 with a stop at say 350, a reward to risk ratio of just 2 to 1, but with a much better chance of success. If risking £200 on the trade the bet in the first case would be £20 a point, (20 times the difference between 400 and 390 is 200) in the second case it would £4 a point (4 times the difference between 400 and 350 is 200). Or one could base the stop and the bet size on ATR, as discussed in the chapter on this subject.

Antofagasta

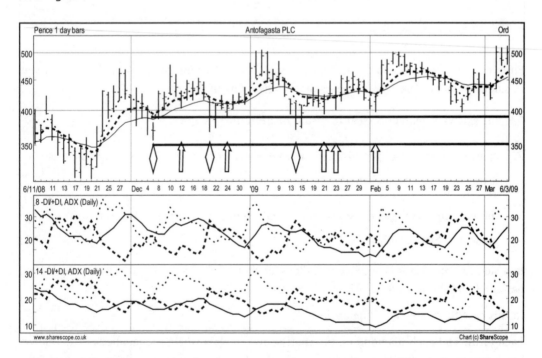

As it happens either trade structure would have been successful, as we can see by moving ahead in time. On this chart I have also added two horizontal lines to show the two levels of support discussed above.

The basic principles for taking trades based on resistance on a sideways market are exactly the same as for taking trades based on support.

Uptrend

This next chart is a great illustration that the game of trading is not easy, and that the trader is frequently called upon to interpret conflicting evidence. Look at the ADX indicator and the moving averages, and then look for fractals representing both support and resistance. Ideally without looking ahead see if you could see a potential trade in the stock Hochschild Mining. Make sure you can list as many reasons to go long or to go short as possible, with any contra indications you can find. The latest closing price is 142p.

Hochschild Mining

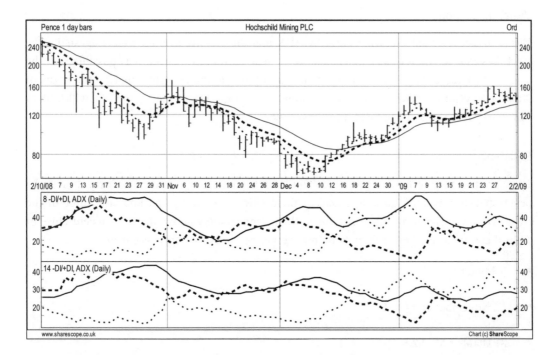

At the time the overall market was in a wide volatile trading range (not illustrated) and was below the mid point of this trading range but not at the bottom. The picture for the mining sector looked similar. This background did not rule out long or short trades in individual stocks.

Let's analyse this stock looking in turn at ADX, moving averages, visual inspection, resistance and support. We can then draw a conclusion and structure a trade. For those that like to know what happened we also show the outcome.

ADX

The 14 day ADX was in downtrend mode for the first half of the chart, but on 18 December 2008 the +DI line crossed the –DI. From 31 December to the end of the chart the 14 day ADX has been in uptrend mode (above 20 and rising, with +DI above –DI) and the 8 day ADX has been above 25.

Moving averages

For the first half of the chart the moving average combination was in downtrend mode. On 15 December it moved into sideways mode as the 4 day average crossed up over the 9 day. From 24 December to the end of the chart the moving average combination has been in uptrend mode (4 above 9 and 9 above 18). The most recent pullback has caused the 4 day to turn down and the 9 day to go flat.

Visual inspection

Visual inspection confirms what both the ADX and the moving average tool suggested – the stock has moved from a clear downtrend to a clear uptrend. However, it is possible that the stock is forming a wide trading range with the top of the range represented by the highs of 3 and 4 November, in which case we are now close to the top of that range. We will look at this more closely under the heading of resistance.

Resistance

There are two very recent fractals at 157 and 160. If going long we could wait for these to be penetrated, or we could go long ahead of them being penetrated and hope the force of the trend will be sufficient to lift prices above them. Immediately above the most recent close of 142p there are a number of fractals before we get as far as the most recent ones:

- 6 January at 143.5

- 12 November at 143.25

- 21 October at 152.5

Also of potential importance is a fractal which represented very brief support in the previous downtrend, the one on 8 October at 154.5.

If all these resistance levels are penetrated there are still two further major hurdles for price to get through, the fractal at 171.5 (3 November) and the one at 188.5 (14 October). However it is possible we can structure the trade so we can still get a good reward-to-risk ratio even if price doesn't get through that 188.5 hurdle.

Some traders would look at all that resistance and go in search of a trade with less obvious difficulties.

Support

There is recent support for current prices in the form of two fractals:

- 131.75 on 23 January

- 134.5 on 29 January

In addition, if price tomorrow were to hold above today's low of 135.75, then since yesterday's low was higher than 135.75 we would have a *new* fractal at 135.75.

Before we move on to the conclusion here is a revised chart showing the fractals mentioned. Diamonds are use to show fractals providing resistance and arrows to show fractals providing support. In addition some horizontal lines have been drawn on to the chart at certain key levels. Remember, this involves interpretation, you may not agree with my interpretation.

Hochschild Mining

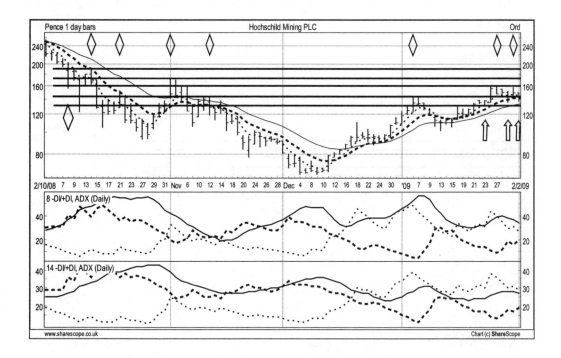

Conclusion – the trade

A lot of resistance above the latest close – true. No way of knowing if the trade is going to work – also true. But in favour of a long trade now:

1. Both the ADX and the moving average tools, confirmed by visual inspection, say price is currently in an uptrend.

2. If today's low holds tomorrow we have a clear place to put a stop, below the lowest of the previous two fractals, and we will have a third fractal confirming this support zone.

3. We can bet in effect that support will hold and enter the trend to see whether or not it can overcome the various resistance levels.

1 ATR in this stock stood at this point at 13 (not shown). Near the close of play the next day it was clear that there was going to be a higher low. With price near 144.0 a 1 ATR stop could be set at 131, below the previous two fractals.

The outcome

This final chart shows the position about a month later. I have left in all the diamonds, arrows and lines drawn up until the trade was taken. Just how much profit was taken on this trade

Hochschild Mining

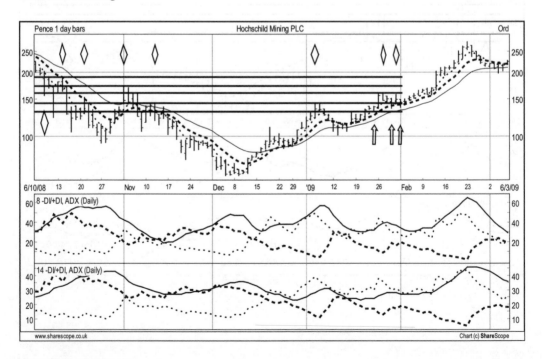

would have depended on what kind of exit methodology was used. Price during this subsequent period reached a peak of 278.25p, 134.25p above the entry price, representing a profit of over ten times the original risk.

Note: The most successful trades are not always comfortable to take.

Downtrend

Here is a trade which a lot of traders missed, and which shows that to be successful some flexibility of interpretation is often needed. It is a chart of the key US index the S&P 500. There was much speculation at the time that we were close to a low and the index was due a large rebound.

S&P 500

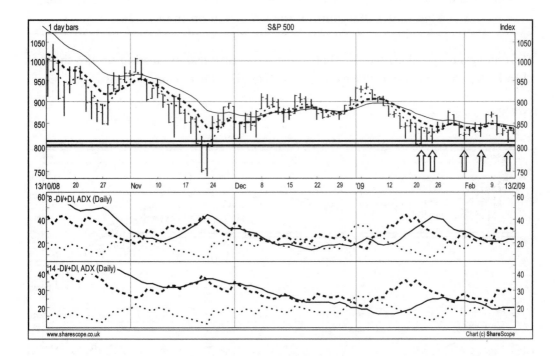

Visual inspection did give some impression that a base was being formed after the declines in the earlier part of 2008. Five recent fractals in late January and early February seemed to offer some support in a zone just above 800 (marked with arrows), and there were further fractals around this level going back to November and December (the one penetration of this level in late November was met with frantic buying which immediately pushed price back above the level).

Given the index was at one of its lowest levels in a decade there were some traders ready to press the buy button.

But both the ADX tool and the moving average combination were in downtrend mode, so it was worth further thought. If price broke down through all that support everyone banking on it would be in losing trade; support would potentially become resistance. Some traders resolved to go short if price fell below 800, with a stop above that support zone, around 820.

History records that that short trade was an excellent trade to take, but those who had originally planned to go long at the support needed to be flexible and rethink the situation.

Fractals can be used once in a trade to provide the location for trailing stops, and the short trade in the S&P 500 is a good example of how this can work. Every time the index made a lower fractal than the previous one the stop could be moved to a little above the most recent fractal.

> *Note*: It is usually best to allow a little bit of space between the fractal and the stop rather than putting the stop bang on the fractal.

The trailing stop positions for this short trade in the S&P 500 are marked on this updated chart by the short black line above each new fractal. The day of entry is circled.

S&P 500

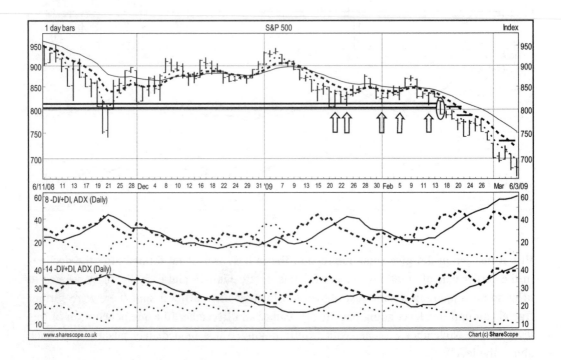

Alternatives

There are no obvious alternative tools in this area.

Conclusion

This is a critical area for traders. Almost every successful trader has some knowledge of support and resistance and will be able to identify key support and resistance levels in the time frame being traded.

TOOL 5: OSCILLATORS

Background and construction

Oscillators have been in use for many decades – many of them were born in the era when the programmable calculator, and then after that the personal computer, came into existence, making the various calculations which most of them perform relatively straightforward for the trader to take advantage of.

We will look at two specific oscillators:

1. RSI

2. Stochastics

Just before we get into the detail of how these oscillators are constructed let's look at a chart of the FTSE 100 with both RSI and stochastics added. The settings are comparable – we will look at settings in more detail a little later in this chapter.

For the time being just note that there are many similarities in the way that the two oscillators respond to price action. When RSI is at a relatively high level, most of the time so is the stochastics indicator. When RSI is at a relatively low level, most of the time so is the stochastics indicator. Some traders like to have both displayed on their charts, rather than just picking one of them to use, but the added value of this is often limited. We will look at the interpretation of these two oscillators later in the chapter.

RSI and stochastics – FTSE 100

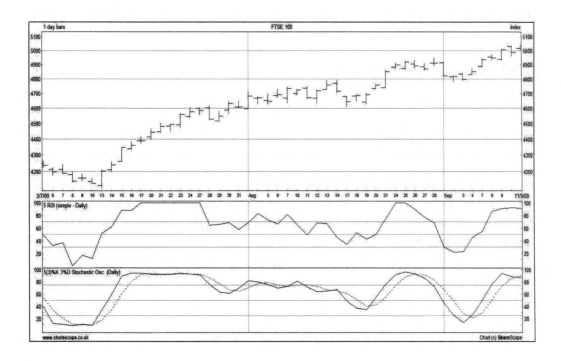

1. RSI

This is an oscillator first presented to the world in Welles Wilder's book *New Concepts in Technical Trading Systems*. RSI is short for Relative Strength Index. It is a *banded* oscillator, which means it has defined lower and upper limits. Its lower limit is zero and its upper limit is 100. The interpretation is generally:

- Zero to 30 is taken as an *oversold* zone,

- 70 to 100 is an *overbought* zone.

RSI looks at closing prices over a user-defined period and compares the value of up closes to the value of down closes–

- An *up close* is a day where the close is higher than the previous close, and the value used in the calculations is simply the difference between that close and the previous close.

- A *down close* is a day where the close is lower than the previous close.

In principle (although it is slightly more complex than this), a series of up closes throughout the period with no down closes would produce a reading on the oscillator of 100; a series of down closes throughout the period with no up closes would produce a reading on the oscillator of 0.

Almost all charting packages include RSI, so there should be no need to do the calculation oneself, but for interest the basic formula to calculate it is:

RSI = 100 – (100 divided by (1 + RS))

where,

RS = average of up closes divided by average of down closes over the user-defined period.

In the original version Welles Wilder introduced a shortcut for updating the RSI value from one period to another (before personal computer days remember). For a 14 day RSI the short cut was to take the most recent RSI value and multiply it by 13, then add today's RSI value, then divide the total by 14.

ShareScope software allows you to select from three methods of calculation:

1. the Welles Wilder method (as above),

2. a simple version without the Welles Wilder shortcut, and

3.   a version which uses exponential averages.

I haven't found it makes a huge difference which version I use, and I tend to just select the simple version.

2. Stochastics

The Stochastics oscillator looks at where the most recent closing price is relative to the range of closing prices over a user-defined period. There are actually two types of Stochastics, one called *Fast Stochastics*, the other called *Slow Stochastics*. Most traders prefer Slow Stochastics, and that is the type that is usually used in charting packages.

There are two lines in the Stochastics oscillator, referred to as %K and %D.

%K is calculated as:

> (this period's close minus the lowest low in the user-defined number of periods) divided by (the highest high in the user-defined number of periods less the lowest low in the user-defined number of periods) expressed as a percentage

In the Slow Stochastics version the figures obtained through this calculation are then averaged over a user-defined number of periods (to smooth the data).

Once %K has been obtained, %D is just an average of %K, again with the user defining the number of periods to be used in the averaging process.

So let us take the example of a 12,3,3 Stochastic. The first figure, 12, represents the number of periods that the oscillator looks at to calculate the high-low range with which to compare the most recent closing price. The second figure, 3, is the number of periods used to create %K; so in this case %K is a 3 period moving average of the raw data. The third figure, in this case also 3, represents the number of periods used to take a moving average of %K to produce %D.

Moving averages in these calculations are usually either simple or exponential – exponential tends to be the most popular choice.

Overview of tool

An oscillator is a special type of indicator which, as the name suggests, oscillates from one extreme to the other, based on price action. Most oscillators have a defined range of values, often from zero to 100.

The basic theory behind oscillators is that, whether the overall trend is up, down or sideways, price action tends to fluctuate around an overall central tendency, and that these fluctuations tend to go from one extreme to another in a natural ebb and flow.

So, goes the theory, whatever the overall direction, there will be times when price has moved relatively high, and other times when price has moved relatively low. Analysts label these times *overbought* and *oversold* respectively. In certain circumstances such overbought or oversold conditions can assist with identification of low risk entries to trades, or with identification of potential exit points.

A number of the oscillators once constructed then also lend themselves to further analysis, for instance:

- Some analysts look for specific patterns in specific oscillators which they believe have predictive power.

- Some analysts draw trend lines on specific oscillators, with a break of a trend line carrying significance.

- Differences between the behaviour of the oscillator and the behaviour of prices are considered significant, for instance if price makes a higher high but the oscillator makes a lower high some would see as a warning sign that an uptrend is losing momentum.

Strengths of oscillators

The strengths of this type of tool are:

- when banded, provide an objective indication of potential price extremes,

- easily programmed and therefore available in many investment/trading software programs,

- applicable on all time frames,

- long pedigree (both in general, and many of the specific oscillators), and

- oscillators tend to be leading indicators, as opposed to lagging indicators, and can therefore be used to anticipate price action.

Weaknesses of oscillators

The weaknesses of this type of tool are:

- some of the oscillators tend to be over-used (particularly the better known ones) and used inappropriately, regarded as panaceas for all trading problems,

- oscillators tend to work well in sideways markets or when used to take trades in line with the prevailing trend, but tend to work poorly if the trader uses them to go against the prevailing trend.

Settings

With both RSI and Stochastics there are trade-offs in choosing the settings to use. Lower value settings will be more responsive and will produce more signals, but the signals will tend to be less reliable. Higher value settings will be less responsive and will produce less signals, but the signals will tend to be more reliable.

In his book Welles Wilder used a 14 period setting for RSI, and that is a popular choice with many traders. 9 is also a popular choice and 5 is also used. I sometimes use a setting as low as 3 but only when identifying possible opportunities to enter a strong trend. At the higher end of the scale I am aware of some traders using 21 as a setting.

Popular settings for Stochastics include:

- 21,3,3

- 12,3,3

- 9,3,3

- 5,3,3

> *Note*: It is quite common to use the same number both to average %K and to produce %D.

Successful traders who use this particular tool generally find it is best to pick one or either of these two oscillators and stick with it, rather than use them side by side. The charts in this chapter will use either a 5 period RSI or a 5,3,3 stochastic oscillator.

How to use this tool

There are people who use oscillators in this way: whenever the oscillator gets oversold they buy, whenever the oscillator gets overbought they sell short. But this is a very dangerous way to use oscillators. For one simple reason: in an uptrend oscillators can stay at overbought levels for extended periods of time, and selling short can produce extended periods of losses. Similarly, in a downtrend oscillators can stay at oversold levels for extended periods of time, and buying can produce extended losses.

The best way to use oscillators therefore is to take into account the type of market before using them:

- in an **uptrend** use oscillators only to identify possible opportunities to go *long* (when the oscillator gets oversold),

- in a **downtrend** use oscillators only to identify possible opportunities to go *short* (when the oscillator gets overbought),

- in a **sideways** market *both long and short trades* can be taken (long trades when the oscillator gets oversold, short trades when the oscillator gets overbought).

We look at an example of each of these in the charts below.

My preference is to use oscillators primarily to identify a window of time to enter a trade in the direction of a longer term trend, so if the overall trend is up I wait for a pullback which drives the oscillator into the oversold zone, and if the overall trend is down I wait for a retracement which drives the oscillator into the overbought zone. For timing the entry I then look for specific price action rather than wait for an oscillator signal.

However, you should be aware that there are a range of specific oscillator signals which are used by some traders to generate trades. Very briefly here are a selection of them.

RSI signals

1. Moves up out of oversold zone (from below to above 30), considered *buy* signals.

2. Moves down out of overbought zone (from above to below 70), considered *sell* signals.

3. Chart patterns on the oscillator; some traders draw trend lines on the oscillator and attribute predictive value to a break of the trend line.

4. Geometric patterns – some traders look for patterns such as double tops, triple tops and head and shoulders patterns in the oscillator, to which they attribute predictive value; Welles Wilder himself describes a pattern he calls "The Failure Swing".

5. Divergence – differences between price action and the action of the oscillator are attributed predictive value.

6. Some trades look for breaks of support and resistance drawn on the oscillator, and consider them leading indicators for breaks of support and resistance levels on the price chart.

Stochastic signals

1. Moves up out of oversold zone (from below to above 20), considered *buy* signals.

2. %K crossing %D from below, considered a *buy* signal.

3. Some traders look for both these two signals combined.

4. Moves down out of the overbought zone (from above to below 80), considered *sell* signals.

5. %K crossing %D from above, considered a *sell* signal.

6. Some traders look for both these last two signals combined.

7. Divergence – as for RSI.

8. Line direction – both lines rising considered bullish, look for opportunities to *buy*; both lines falling considered bearish, look for opportunities to *sell*.

Example

We will look at three charts, the first will show a sideways market, and the other two will show how we can use an oscillator in first an uptrend and then a downtrend.

Sideways market

Let us return to the instrument we looked at in the last chapter when selling resistance and buying support in a sideways market. The time period covered is the same, but it now has a 5 period RSI added. Two lines have been drawn on the RSI showing the start of the overbought zone (30) and the start of the oversold zone (70).

Antofagasta

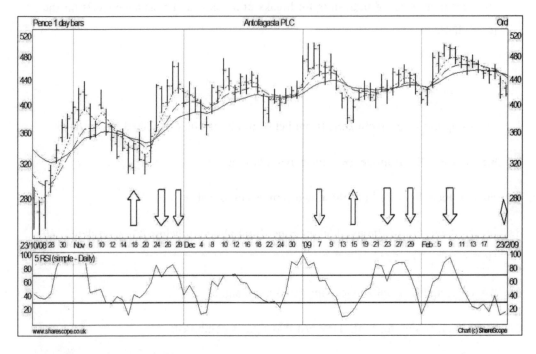

The down arrows show every time price formed a fractal with the middle bar having a higher high than the two outer bars, at the same time as the RSI had reached an overbought reading. Some traders would have seen the overbought reading in the oscillator, would have recognised that the stock was at the upper end of a trading range and would have seen the fractal forming on the third day (with that day setting up to have a lower high). They would have gone short.

The up arrows show every time price formed a fractal with the middle bar having a lower low than the two outer bars, at the same time as the RSI had reached an oversold reading. Some traders would have seen the oversold reading in the oscillator, would have recognised that the stock was at the lower end of a trading range and would have seen the fractal forming on the third day (with that day setting up to have a higher low). They would have gone long.

The diamond shows exactly the same potential entry position as we saw in the last chapter, except we now also have the RSI oscillator at an oversold level.

In each case the oscillator has helped to pinpoint a potential entry. How successful that trade would have been if taken would depend on how the trade was exited – many traders who trade this way will start to lock in profits as soon as they materialise, by trailing a stop; and certainly by the time price nears the other side of the trading range the stop will be very tight.

Note also that a number of the trades would have resulted in the trader being stopped out with a loss. For example, at the very first down arrow the trader would have gone short with a stop above the fractal, and very soon that stop would have been hit.

Uptrend

Here is another trade that required some weighing up of the pros and cons; the instrument was the stock Carpetright PLC.

Carpetright

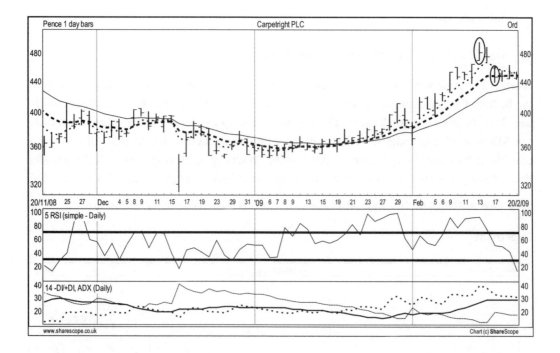

Against taking a long trade in Carpetright were two key factors:

1. Although the FTSE All Share Index (not shown) was still in a wide and volatile trading range, the major US index the S&P 500 (not shown) had moved into downtrend mode, as measured by the ADX indicator; some traders were therefore not interested at this point in any long trades.

2. On 17 January price had opened below the low of the previous day and price never got as high as that low during the day – this was at least for the short term a bearish development (the term for this is a *gap*). In addition there had been another gap, this

time upwards two days before. Such a combination of two gaps after a period of trending prices produced a phenomenon known as an *island reversal*, which after an upmove is a bearish development. The two gap days are circled.

In favour of taking a long trade in Carpetright was:

1. ADX indicator in uptrend mode,

2. moving average combination in uptrend mode,

3. visual inspection shows a powerful uptrend during the period of the second half of the chart, and

4. the RSI oscillator had fallen to oversold levels.

Whether the trade was taken would depend on the overall game plan of the trader. In light of the bearish factors outlined above, however, if a long trade was taken the strategy should have been to aim for a quick profit. The day before the up gap was the middle bar in a fractal, a 1 ATR stop of 22p could have been placed comfortably below that fractal. An entry was possible at the open the next day at around 446p. With a stop at 424p (446 -22) if the trader risked £200 per trade this trade would have been at £9 per point (total risk 22 x 9 = £198).

Look now at the chart two days after the entry to this trade (shown by the up arrow).

Carpetright

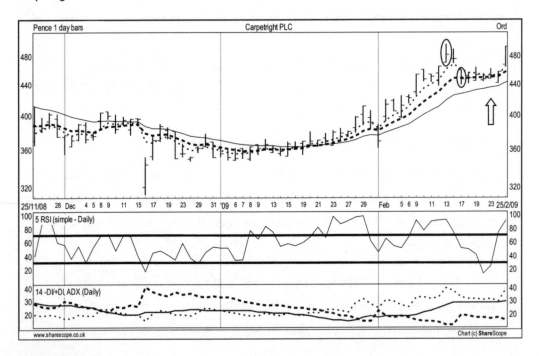

Price had shot up to near the most recent high, and the RSI oscillator had now become overbought. Given the overall market conditions, which were getting more bearish by the day, it would have been a good idea to grab this profit while it lasted. Notice that the island reversal made little impact on this occasion.

An exit at the open the next day was possible around 485p. At £9 per point this would have represented a profit of £351 (485 – 446, times 9). Profit of 1.8 times initial risk is not spectacular, but this was not a time to be holding long trades to capture big moves.

Downtrend

This next chart is another warning to any trader who is hoping that all is required for success is to set up all the tools, find some charts where all the tools give the same message, take the trade and rake in the profits. The reality is that sometimes there are conflicting messages from the various tools in this book, and the trader will need to weigh up and interpret the evidence. Some judgement will be required.

BT Group

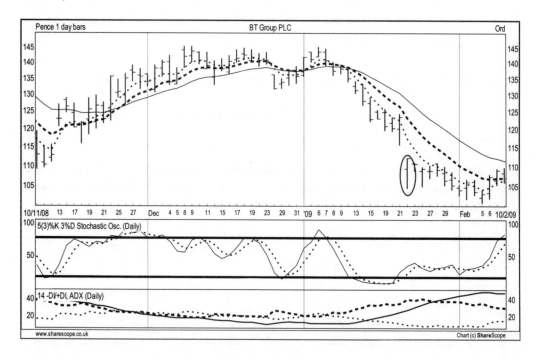

When we discussed the ADX indicator we referred to the requirement that, for the 14 day indicator to be in downtrend mode, it should be at 20 or higher and rising. We also mentioned that one of the signals that can be generated by this indicator is for the ADX line to turn down from above the two DI lines; this is a warning that the trend may be ending.

A trader taking note of the above may well have decided looking at the chart not to investigate a down bet in this stock: the ADX indicator had indeed turned down from above the two DI lines, and was falling. In addition it looked like the 4 day moving average was about to cross up over the 9 day, turning the moving average configuration to sideways mode.

On the other hand, visual inspection does reveal that the stock has been in a powerful downtrend throughout 2009.

On this occasion there are two pieces of evidence which suggest a short trade might be a good bet nonetheless:

1.   the gap down on 22 January (circled), a bearish development; price may well struggle to rise back above that gap, and

2.   the recent three day rally has caused the %K line of the stochastic oscillator to become overbought.

If one concluded that this was a valid setup for a short trade there were various options for getting into the trade:

1.   enter on the open the next day, on the basis of the stochastic oscillator becoming overbought in a downtrend,

2.   wait for the downtrend to reassert itself by falling below the low of the last day,

3.   wait for the downtrend to reassert itself by the next day having a lower high than the last day.

As it happens any of these three techniques would have triggered a potentially very successful down bet, as can be seen by looking at the chart a few weeks later – the day of entry is shown by the down arrow.

BT Group

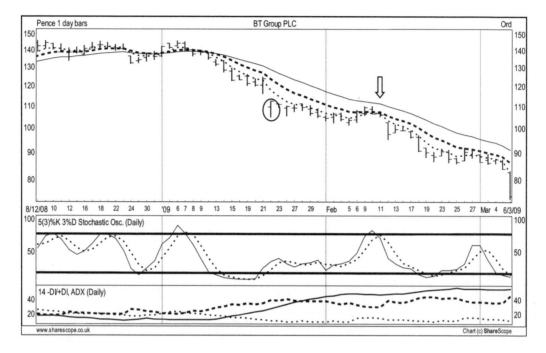

Alternatives

Many traders do very well without oscillators. Others use them initially to assist trading decisions, but then learn to identify good places to enter and exit trades just by looking at price action (visual inspection). I personally tend to use them primarily on intra day charts, for instance on the ten minute and the five minute chart I use for day trading currencies.

It is worth mentioning one more oscillator, created by Larry Williams. It is called Williams %R. Like stochastics it is based on where price has closed in relation to the range of prices over a user-defined period. It has an enthusiastic band of followers, and is well worth considering as an alternative to stochastics.

Conclusion

Oscillators are hugely popular and in my view massively over-used, but there is a role for them in the trader's arsenal. To repeat, my personal preference is to use them primarily on intraday charts (there are many traders looking at them intraday, and some of them will be taking the exact same signals, which in turn means the signals might become self-fulfilling prophecies).

1.7900

1.7855

1.7810

TOOL 6: RELATIVE STRENGTH

05.14

08.47

Background and construction

Relative strength compares one instrument's price movement with another. This can be a useful thing to do whatever the asset class, but the tool really comes into its own when trading stocks.

Here is an interesting chart of the FTSE 350 Pharmaceuticals and Biotechnology sector for a six month period from early March 2009. The sector was in a steady uptrend, but it clearly wasn't the best way to enjoy the market rally during the period, as can be seen by looking at the indicator showing its relative performance to the FTSE 100. This shows that the sector underperformed the FTSE 100 by 11% over the period.

Relative strength – FTSE 350 Pharmaceuticals and Biotechnology sector

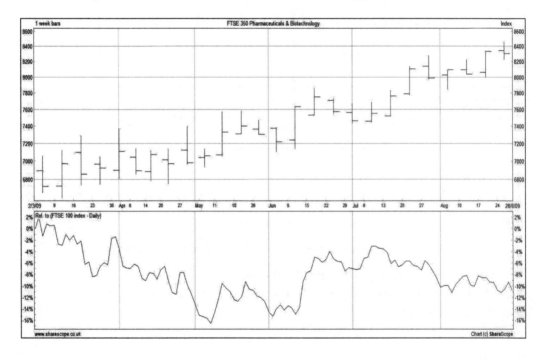

Here is an easy way to grasp what we really mean when we say that a sector has underperformed or over-performed the market, or that at a stock has underperformed or over performed the market or its sector by a certain amount. Let us take the example of a sector index underperforming the overall market by say 5%. This means that for the period being considered if we bought an equal monetary amount of the sector and of the overall market index on day one of the period being considered, on the last day of the period being considered our investment in the sector index would have been worth 5% less than our investment in the overall market index.

Here is a simplified example.

	Day 1	Last day	Difference
Price of Market Index	1000	1200	+200
Value of £10,000 investment in Market Index	£10,000	£12,000	+£2000
Price of Sector Index	500	570	+70
Value of £10,000 investment in Sector Index	£10,000	£11,400	+£1140

Difference between end value of sector investment and market index = £11,400 - £12,000 = -£600

-£600 divided by end value of market index, £12,000 = -5%

Therefore, the sector index has underperformed market index by 5% over the period.

Remember, we are comparing the *relative* performance of one instrument with another. They might both go down over the period, but if one goes down less than the other it has *outperformed* the other.

Overview of tool

A key assumption underlying this tool is that over-performance or underperformance of one instrument versus another can trend, just as the underlying prices can trend. The purpose of the tool is to identify such under or over-performance with a view to capitalising on its tendency to persist.

Strengths of relative strength

The strengths of the tool include:

•   conceptually straightforward,

- long pedigree,

- easily programmed and therefore available on many trading software packages, and

- easily incorporated into existing trading strategies as a filter for selection of trading candidates.

Weaknesses of relative strength

I am not aware of any weaknesses.

Construction

This is a very simple tool. For a user-defined period the change in price of one instrument is compared with the change in price of the other, and usually expressed as a percentage. (In the ShareScope program the user has the option of either having this percentage plotted on the price chart, or having it plotted beneath the price chart as a separate indicator.)

Settings

The key decisions required from the trader when using relative strength for stock trading are:

1. which instrument to use for comparison purposes,

2. over what time frame to compare the two instruments, and

3. what level of out/underperformance to look for.

Two key instruments to compare a stock to are the stock's sector and the overall market. One possible choice in the UK for the overall market is to use the FTSE All Share Index. Some traders trading just FTSE 100 stocks might select the FTSE 100 Index instead, but for those trading a range of stocks of varying sizes it is important to note that the FTSE 100 will itself at times over or under-perform the All Share Index, so the All Share would be preferable.

The time frame to use for the comparison will be partly determined by the type of trading favoured by the trader. For instance if the trader is typically only in a trade for a few days to a few weeks then outperformance or underperformance over say the last month is probably of most interest. Those whose trades typically last three months or longer might be more interested in a longer time frame for the comparison, for example three months.

The level of out/underperformance sought will vary from period to period, depending on the number of trading candidates it produces. A useful starting point is usually 10% for out/under performance of the overall market.

How to use this tool

There are many ways to use this tool. For me, the most important by far is as part of a top-down process for selecting trading candidates. The charts in this chapter focus exclusively on this process. However the tool can also be used to make pairs trades. And some traders look for specific patterns in the plotted relative strength line.

Top-down selection

The methodology here is simple but powerful.

- If the intention is to go **long,** first identify those sectors which are outperforming the overall index. Then identify stocks which are outperforming the sector, or at least not underperforming it.

- If the intention is to go **short,** first identify those sectors which are underperforming the overall index. Then identify stocks which are underperforming the sector, or at least not out performing it.

Pairs trades

There are many different ways to take pairs trades. Most involve identifying two instruments whose performance normally has a degree of correlation (e.g. the companies BP and Shell). Then a common technique is to wait until their relative performance has reached an extreme level compared with the long-term relationship (one instrument significantly underperforming, the other overperforming), and then bet that the relative performance will revert to the mean (the overperformer will start underperforming and the underperformer will start overperforming).

I tend to adopt an opposite technique: I take two stocks from the same sector, one outperforming the sector, the other underperforming it and go long the first and short the second. Net exposure both to the market and to the sector should be nearly zero, and the trade will be successful if the outperformance and underperformance continue.

Specific patterns

Some traders use traditional technical analysis techniques on the relative strength chart itself. The more common techniques are to look for:

1. geometric patterns, such as double tops and bottoms, head and shoulder patterns etc,

2.   breakouts from consolidation areas,

3.   trend line breaks.

In each case the assumption is that action on the relative strength chart is a precursor to action on the price chart.

Example

The chart examples illustrate a top down approach for identifying trading candidates in the stock market. The principles are applicable to any stock market.

Note that this tool generally works best when the overall market is trending:

- in a **downtrend**, find the underperforming sectors, then the underperforming stocks in those sectors,

- in an **uptrend**, find the outperforming sectors, then the underperforming stocks in those sectors.

In a sideways market it is possible to run a long/short portfolio based on relative strength, however for many traders it is better to stand aside and wait for a new trend in the overall market.

The analysis in this example is as at 6 June 2008. In this case, since we have a downtrend, we are looking for underperformance. We select 10% underperformance as our benchmark.

The logical progression for identifying outperformance when the overall market is in an uptrend is similar: from overall market to sector, from sector to individual stocks.

Overall market

FTSE All Share Index

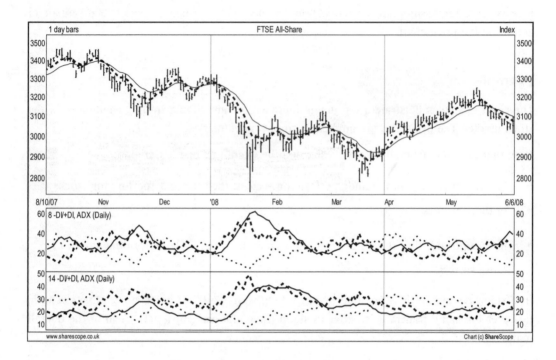

Visual inspection of the All Share Index shows the following:

1. a decline of over 20% from late October 2007 to January 2008,

2. a sideways market from January to March 2008,

3. a retracement of the previous downtrend from March to May 2008, peaking on 19 May,

4. a new move down starting 20 May, causing both the moving average combination and the ADX indicator to transition into downtrend mode.

Underperforming sectors

At this point, the sectors underperforming the overall market by at least 10% over the previous month were:

*   Automobiles and parts

*   Banks

FTSE Automobiles and Parts

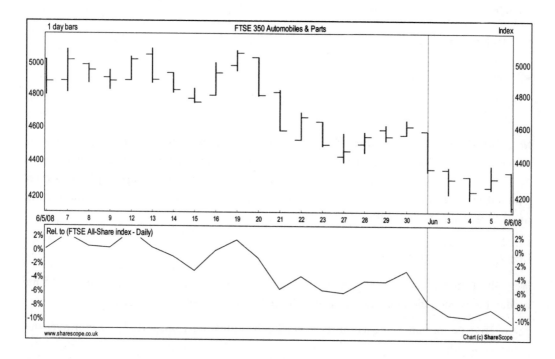

FTSE Banks

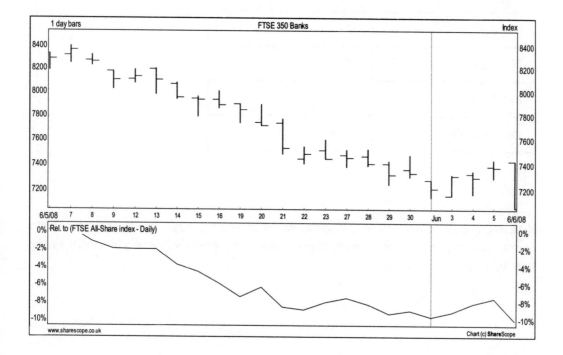

Those underperforming the overall market by less than 10% but over 5% (not illustrated) included:

- Forestry and paper

- Industrial transportation

- Real estate

Note that at various points during 2008 and 2009 there were restrictions on short selling in certain sectors, primarily financial sectors, so some sectors and some trading candidates were off limits for a down bet. This meant at certain times sectors underperforming by less than 10% but by more than 5% were used to produce trading candidates, rather than the sectors under performing by more than 10%.

Underperforming stocks

We will illustrate the move from sector analysis to identification of potential trading candidates in the individual stocks within the Industrial Transportation sector.

The relative performance of each of these versus the Industrial Transportation sector over the previous month was:

Stock	Performance
BBA Aviation PLC	–2%
Fisher (James) & Sons PLC	+8%
Forth Ports PLC	–1%
Wincanton PLC	–10%

Here is the chart of one of these, Wincanton, for illustrative purposes. The indicator shows performance versus the overall market; performance versus the sector is represented by the line on the price chart itself.

Wincanton

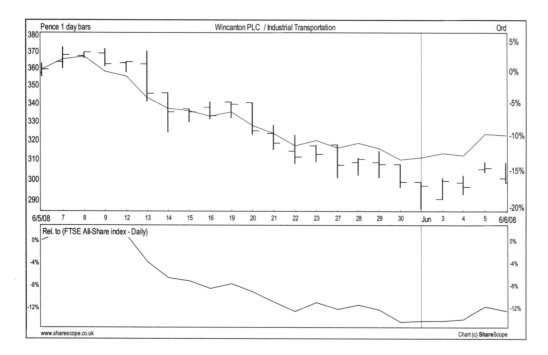

If one was considering a down bet in the Industrial Transportation sector around this period it was logical to first examine the stock which was underperforming the sector by the most.

> *Note*: By late October this stock had halved in price.

Alternatives

For those that like to use point and figure charts, some software packages allow the user to plot relative strength in point and figure format as well as price. All the standard point and figure techniques can be used on the relative strength chart as well as on the price chart. Traders using this technique might for instance trade various types of breakout from a consolidation area on the relative strength chart.

Conclusion

For stock trading this technique is invaluable. In a bull market it helps identify the strongest stocks in the strongest sectors. In a bear market it helps identify the weakest stocks in the weakest sectors. In a sideways market it allows the trader to hold a long and a short portfolio if desired, chosen from outperforming and underperforming sectors.

1.7900

1.7855

1.7810

TOOL 7: MOMENTUM

05.14

08.47

Background and construction

The Momentum indicator, and its close relative the Rate of Change indicator, are really a type of oscillator; nevertheless I have given them a separate chapter. The oscillators we looked at before were banded oscillators and can be used in the way described in that chapter.

If you recall, *banded* means having predefined minimum and maximum values, as for instance in the case of both RSI and the stochastic indicator where the minimum value for the indicators is zero and the maximum value 100. The Momentum and Rate of Change indicators are *unbanded* (i.e. they have no predefined minimum and maximum values) and lend themselves to one specialist technique in particular – *divergence* – which is the focus of attention in this chapter.

We will be examining the concept of divergence in more detail later in the chapter, and how to trade it, but by way of introduction here is a chart of the FTSE 100 showing clear divergence between price action and indicator action in March 2009, which led to a powerful rally.

Momentum – FTSE 100

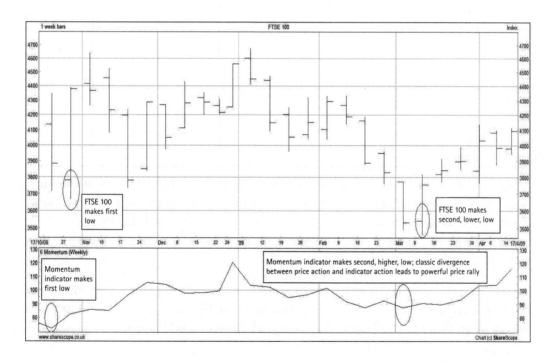

People sometimes refer to the Rate of Change indicator as the Momentum indicator, although technically they are different. Both compare the latest closing price of an instrument to a close X periods ago, where X is defined by the user. The momentum indicator subtracts one from the other, whereas the Rate of Change indicator divides one by the other. This makes little difference unless the difference between the two prices is large. Throughout this chapter, and in the chart examples, the indicator will be based on the division technique.

Note: in the ShareScope package the indicator we will be using is labelled *Momentum* and it uses the division technique.

The indicator we use in this chapter is of fairly simple construction. The latest closing price is divided by the closing price X periods ago (where X is defined by the user) and then expressed as a percentage.

Here is a simple example to illustrate this. In this example the user-defined look back period is 10 periods.

Day	Closing price 10 periods ago (A)	Latest closing price (B)	B divided by A (expressed as a percentage)
1	98	101	103.1
2	99	103	104.0
3	100	105	105.0

Note: The actual indicator reading for each day will be the value calculated in the final column. Note also that although prices were increasing 10 periods ago, they are now increasing at an even faster rate, and therefore the momentum indicator is rising.

Overview of tool

We will be using a specialist technique in respect of this indicator, identifying divergence between price action and indicator action. Although a similar technique can be utilised with banded oscillators, my belief is that it is more effective with this indicator.

Identifying significant turning points

Some analysts use this indicator in other ways, but so far as this book is concerned the purpose of this indicator is to identify potential significant turning points in price when there is divergence between the indicator and price.

The underlying principle here is that before a trend reverses the speed at which prices are moving first slows then comes to a standstill. The momentum indicator measures this speed. The assumption is that changes in the speed (momentum) precede changes in price.

Divergence occurs when price and an indicator are not in synch.

Specifically with momentum divergence we are looking, in a downtrend, for price to make a new low, but momentum not to make a new low. When this happens we have identified a situation where the speed that prices are falling has slowed down. This provides us with a setup for a potential entry to a new trade, and we can define specific requirements for that setup to trigger an actual trade.

In my experience this technique seems to work better for identifying reversals from a downtrend rather than reversals from an uptrend, so in this chapter the example will feature a long trade. In addition, the technique often works better on individual stocks if the sector is also displaying momentum divergence, or is already in an uptrend.

Strengths of momentum

The strengths of this tool, used in this specialist way are:

* the indicator itself is conceptually simple, has a long pedigree, is easily programmable and is available in most trading software,

* divergence techniques are robust and well established and seem to work well with this particular indicator, particularly when trades are taken in line with the sector position,

* can provide an early entry to a new trend, and

* can produce an excellent reward-to-risk ratio, particularly as the overall market moves from down via sideways to up.

Weaknesses of momentum

The weaknesses of this tool, used in this specialist way are:

* tends to work better with longs than shorts,

* technique seems to work more successfully at certain times than at others, so requires some subjective input from the user on when to use it,

- an attempt is being made to enter a new uptrend almost before a downtrend is over; there is always therefore the risk that the old downtrend will be renewed – this tool should be studiously avoided unless the trader can rigorously apply appropriate bet size and exit methodologies.

Settings

Common settings for the Momentum and Rate of Change indicators are:

- 10 periods

- 12 periods

- 20 periods

For the specialist way we used the indicator in this chapter settings between 25 and 30 periods are recommended. In the chart examples we will use a setting of 30 periods, on a three month chart.

How to use this tool

The setup for a potential new trade is divergence, as defined in the Construction section above. Using the example of a long trade, the trader then has a range of choices for the trigger to enter the trade:

1. there will be a new fractal low in place on the price chart, one technique is to wait for price to get near that fractal and then take the trade, effectively buying support,

2. the trigger for the trade could be if price rises above the high of the day when divergence was first defined,

3. some traders apply technical analysis to the Momentum indicator itself, for instance looking for it to exceed its most recent high,

4. others wait for price to exceed the most recent fractal high.

The technique we will use, once divergence has been identified, will be to enter on the first close above the high of the third day of the fractal low, with a stop below the fractal low. If that stop would be less than 1 ATR away, then we will place our stop 1 ATR away.

Example

We will look at a case history of a long trade taken in the stock Balfour Beatty, using the specialist techniques we have discussed.

We first look at the stock at the point where divergence started to occur.

Balfour Beatty

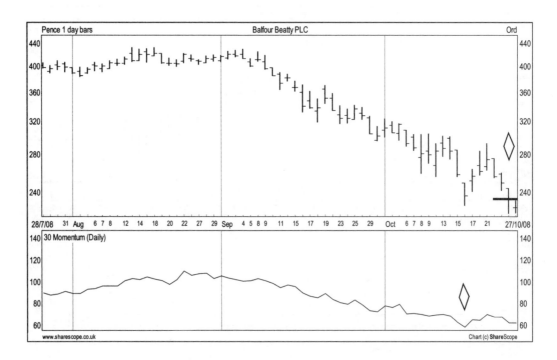

It is clear from visual inspection that the stock has been in a powerful downtrend since early September.

But we have divergence in the Momentum indicator, suggesting the downtrend is losing momentum. The ingredients in this divergence are as follows:

1. price has just made a new low (and a new fractal, three bars with the middle one having a lower low than the two outer ones) – this new low is marked on the price chart with a diamond,

2. but the lowest level on this chart for the Momentum indicator is six days earlier, this low on the Momentum chart is also marked with a diamond, and

3. so there is a new low in price, but a higher low in the Momentum indicator – classic divergence.

Now that we have a divergence setup we wait for the entry trigger – the first close above the high of the third day of the fractal low (i.e. the first close at 231p or higher). A small line has been drawn on the chart at the potential entry level.

Let us move on a couple of days...

Balfour Beatty

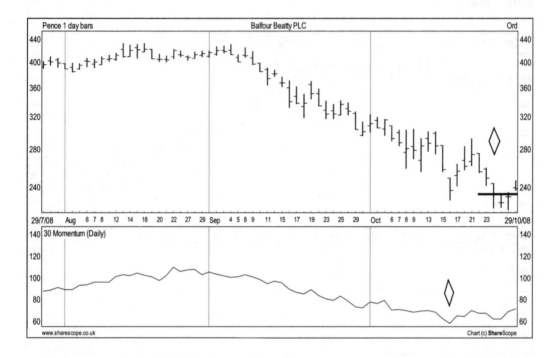

Our entry has been triggered at the close, as price closes at 237.25p. The low of the fractal was 218.75 and the most recent reading for 1 ATR (not shown) is 24p. Since the low of the fractal is less than 1 ATR away we set our stop 1 ATR away (i.e. at 213.25p). If we risk around £200 per trade we will bet £8 per point on this trade, risking £192 (24 x 8).

With this type of trade the minimum target should be twice the amount risked, and in principle the initial stop should not be moved until this minimum target has been reached. We will leave our stop at 213.25p until the price rises to 285.25p (237.25 plus 2 x 24).

The next chart shows when this level was reached, just four days later. The day of entry is marked with an arrow.

Balfour Beatty

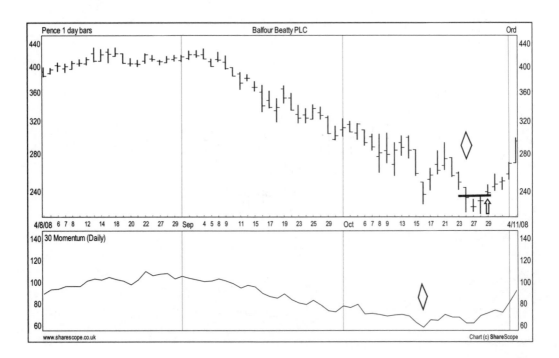

The way forward now will depend on the trader's time frame for trading, risk preferences and objectives. Some traders might have been happy to bag the profit at this point. On the latest day shown the trade could have been closed at the close of play at 293p, a profit of £446, 2.3 times the original risk, just four days later. An alternative approach would have been to move the stop to breakeven, so now the trade cannot lose, and try to ride the new up move for longer. In a sense it is now a free trade.

We now move on a month...

Balfour Beatty

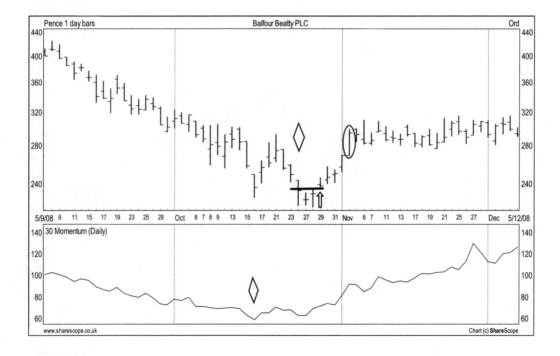

This chart would please those that decided on the quick exit at 293p after four days. One month further on and price closes at 291p. For those that hung on that is a month of funds being tied up in a long trade that has made no further advance. Some traders would have exited during that extra month simply because the trade was not making any progress.

The situation changes three days later...

Balfour Beatty

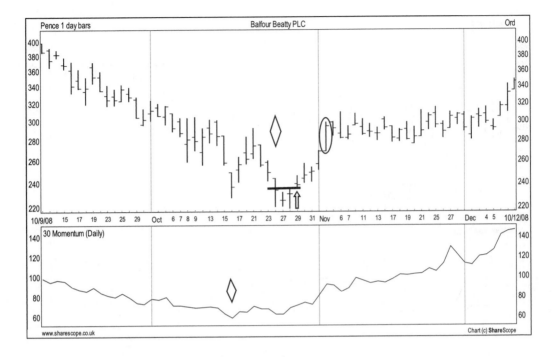

Finally, for those that hung on to this trade, we have a new situation. The stock has moved out of the range it got stuck in for a month. It would be disappointing now to get much less profit than was possible by exiting after just four days, so one sensible course of action would be to move the stop to lock in a profit of twice the original risk (i.e. to move the stop to 285.25p). If price moved down to 285.25 it would mean that it had fallen back into that old trading range, a sign of weakness.

A new development occurs in early January...

Balfour Beatty

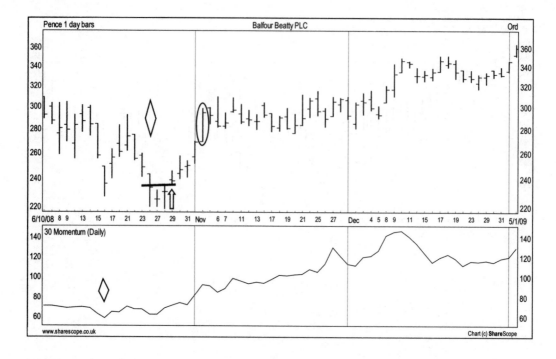

The new development is that price has moved up out of the most recent trading range and in the process has created a gap (the low of today is above the high of yesterday). If that gap is a genuine sign of renewed strength price should not fall back below the gap. We can now move our stop to the bottom of the gap (344p).

Eventually our stop is hit, as can be seen in the next chart.

Balfour Beatty

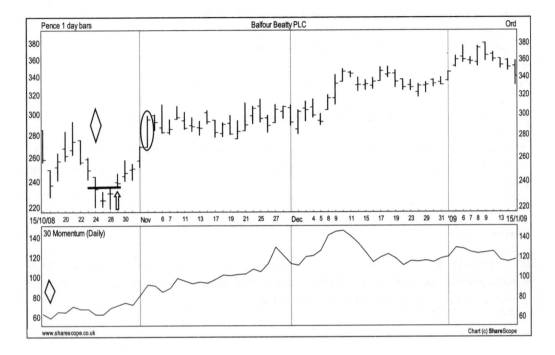

Our eventual profit on this trade was £854, 4.4 times the original risk. If we had somehow managed to exit at the exact high price of the whole up move since our entry we would have had a profit of £1126, 5.9 times the original risk. The first £446 of our profit was achieved in just 4 days, the remaining £408 took more than two months more. Whether that was acceptable or not depends once again on the trader's time frame for trading, risk preferences and objectives.

Alternatives

Alternative techniques for obtaining early entry to a new trend include:

1. moving average techniques, including crossovers,

2. breakout strategies, for instance buying a new 55 day high, and

3. point and figure techniques on both price and relative strength charts.

Some traders use divergence techniques in similar ways to those described but with other oscillators. A number of writers have extolled the virtues of divergence techniques using MACD.

Conclusion

The techniques in this chapter are only for those with robust bet size and exit techniques. It is much easier to identify an existing trend and join it, than to try to capture a new trend at the beginning while managing the associated risk.

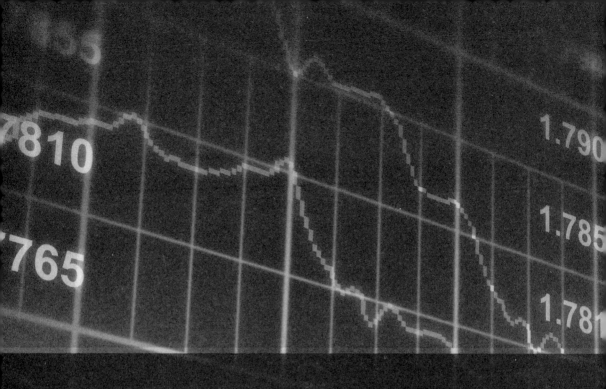

CASE STUDIES

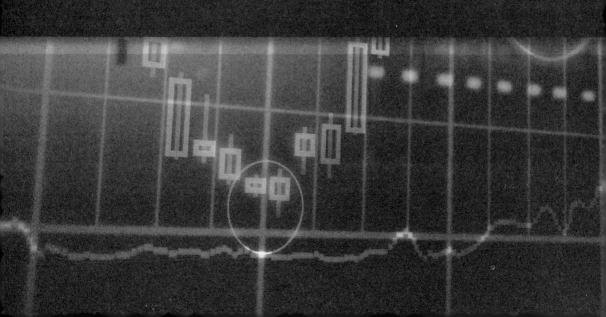

Throughout this book, once a new tool has been introduced it has often been used in subsequent chapters. An incremental approach has therefore been adopted to the introduction of new techniques.

This chapter completes that process by looking at one more trade which draws on a range of the techniques discussed previously.

Each chart will be shown twice. The first time with no commentary – try to form your own opinions on the chart using the tools and techniques we have discussed in the book. Then turn over the page to see the chart once more with my commentary – see if you agree or not with it or not.

We start by looking at the overall market at the end of the third quarter of 2008. Don't turn the page until you have formed an opinion on the chart.

FTSE All Share

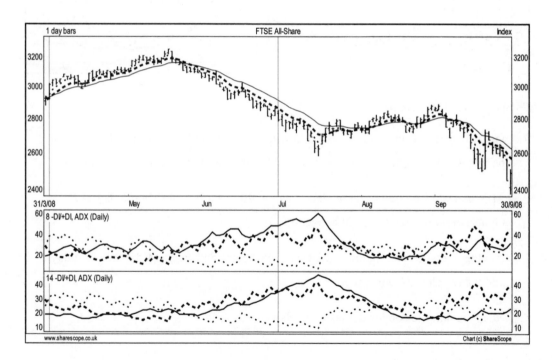

FTSE All Share

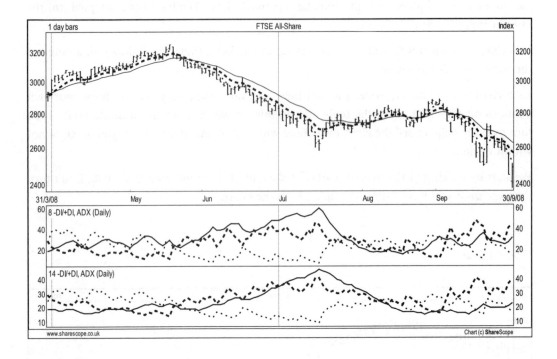

Commentary on this chart:

1. visual inspection reveals a powerful downtrend from mid May to mid July, then a period of retracement, followed by a renewal of the downtrend from early September;

2. ADX indicator in downtrend mode: 14 day at 20 or more and rising; 8 day at 25 or higher; in both cases with +DI above –DI;

3. moving average combination now clearly in downtrend mode (4 day below 9 day and 9 day below 18 day); and

4. we are looking for opportunities to go short.

> Don't forget to check whatever the tools are telling you against the common sense yardstick of visual inspection.

Next, a sector chart...

FTSE 350 Industrial Engineering

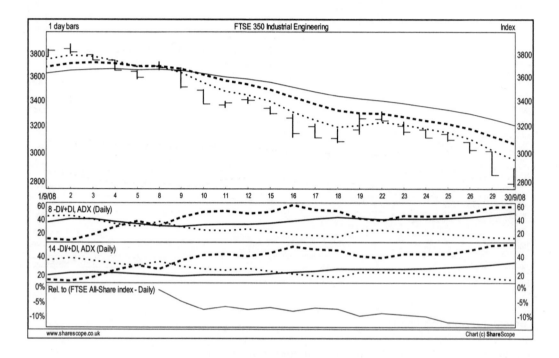

FTSE 350 Industrial Engineering

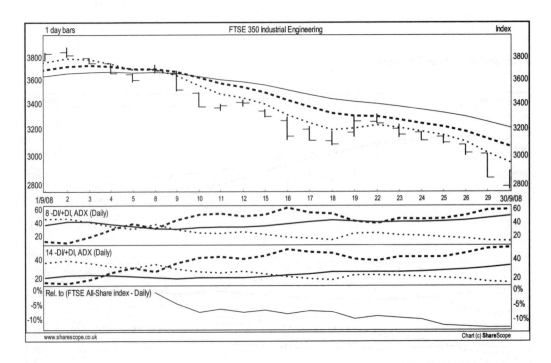

Commentary on this chart:

1. visual inspection reveals a downtrend during the month;

2. ADX indicator in downtrend mode: 14 day at 20 or more and rising; 8 day at 25 or higher; in both cases with +DI above –DI;

3. moving average combination clearly in downtrend mode (4 day below 9 day and 9 day below 18 day);

4. the sector has underperformed the overall market by over 12% over the last month;

5. we are looking for opportunitities to go short in this sector.

If you are comfortable with these conclusions, form a view on the next chart, IMI...

IMI 1

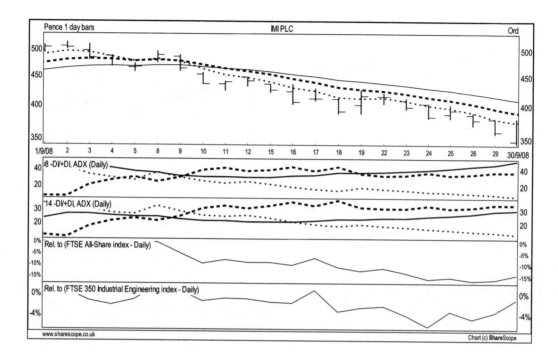

IMI 1

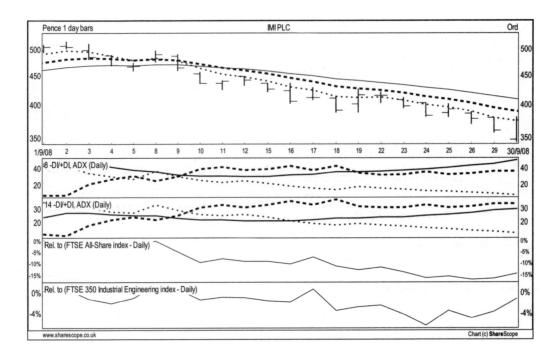

Commentary on this chart:

1. visual inspection reveals a downtrend during the month;

2. ADX indicator in downtrend mode: 14 day at 20 or more and rising; 8 day at 25 or higher; in both cases with +DI above –DI;

3. moving average combination clearly in downtrend mode (4 day below 9 day and 9 day below 18 day);

4. the stock has marginally underperformed its sector over the previous month;

5. the stock has underperformed the overall market by nearly 15% in the month;

6. we will be keen to go short in this stock, so we add it to our shortlist of trading candidates and will start to look for appropriate entry points.

If you are with me so far, now look at the next chart of IMI to identify a possible entry point.

IMI 2

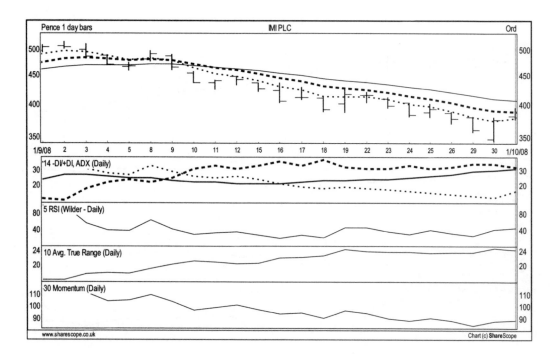

IMI 2

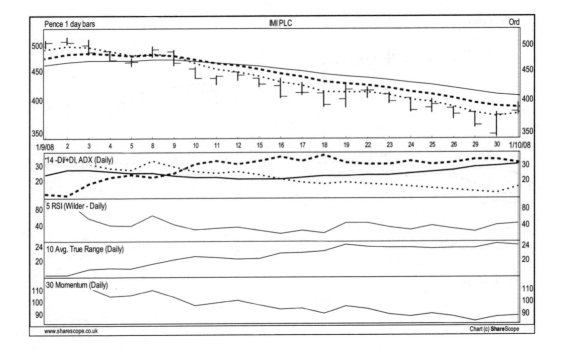

Commentary on this chart:

1. RSI not yet overbought;

2. only one day of a pullback so far;

3. many traders would not yet see a setup on this chart;

4. but be aware that some traders would see a setup simply because the stock has taken out the high of several days; the trigger to enter would be if the stock now takes out the low of today.

The next chart shows the position one day later.

What is your opinion now?

IMI 3

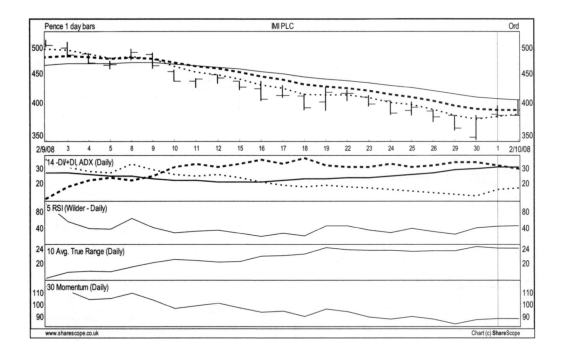

IMI 3

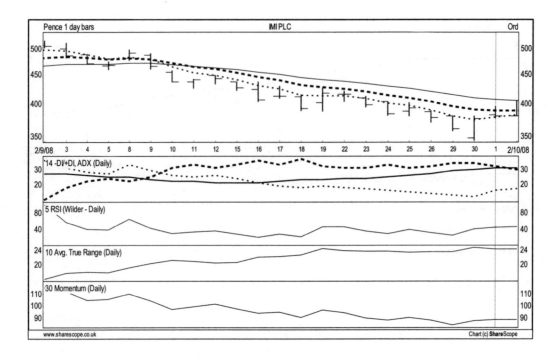

Commentary on this chart:

1. even if we saw a setup yesterday it wasn't triggered today (yesterday's low not taken out);

2. a two day pullback is enough for many traders to see a setup – they will go short tomorrow if price falls below today's low;

3. the RSI followers still don't have a setup – the indicator is not yet overbought.

The next chart shows the position one day later.

What is your opinion now?

IMI 4

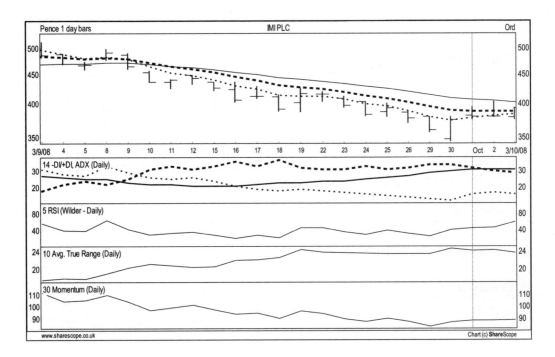

IMI 4

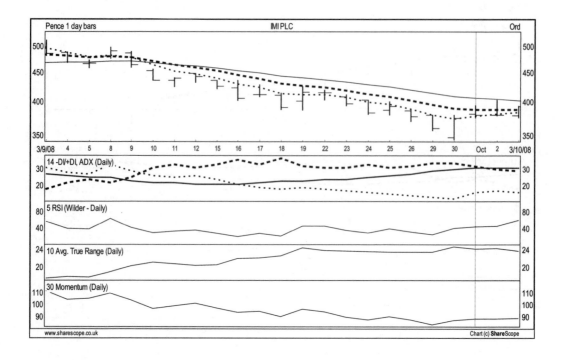

Commentary on this chart:

1. If you decided that you had a setup yesterday you are now in the trade because price went below yesterday's low.

2. If you are in the trade did you automatically think: where is my stop going, how much am I going to risk on this trade, and as a result what is my bet size going to be? If you worked out where your stop should be, did you check to see how far that would be in ATR terms, and whether you were comfortable with that? The right answer to each of these questions will depend on your time frame for trading, risk preferences and objectives, so I am not going to tell you what your special answer should be. The essential thing is that you automatically thought about the issues when you considered your potential entry point.

If you are not in this trade yet, what are you looking for now?

The RSI traders are probably not yet in this trade.

We are now going to fast forward four days. See if your methods would have got you into the trade so far. If not, what is your latest thinking on whether you want to be in this trade or not, and if you do what entry point can you see?

IMI 5

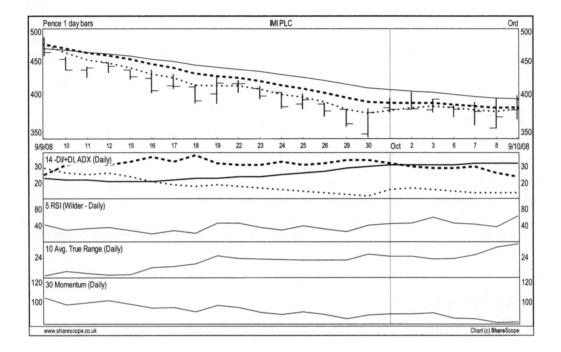

IMI 5

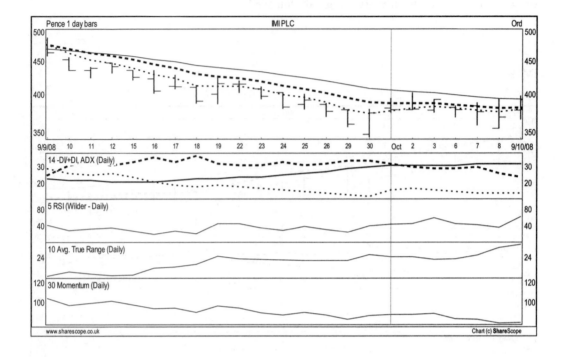

Commentary on this chart:

- both the ADX tool and the moving average combination are still in downtrend mode;

- visual inspection suggests the stock is consolidating slightly;

- there is no divergence in the momentum indicator, this would suggest the momentum of the decline has not yet subsided;

- RSI not very overbought, so no setup yet for the RSI traders;

- there is potential resistance in the form of the fractal which formed on 2 October; three bars where the middle bar had a higher high than the two outer bars;

- if tomorrow's high is lower than today's high we will have another fractal at a very similar level to the 2 October fractal;

- above the two fractals would be a good place to put a stop, and with a good place for a stop we can enter a short trade.

Make sure you have thought about stops (taking into account ATR) and bet size.

Sorry RSI traders, you missed this one.

We are about to move on six days. Even if you didn't get into this trade, imagine you did. How you are going to get out? What are your rules? Trailing stop? Get out on a target? If you use a trailing stop, how do you calculate it?

IMI 6

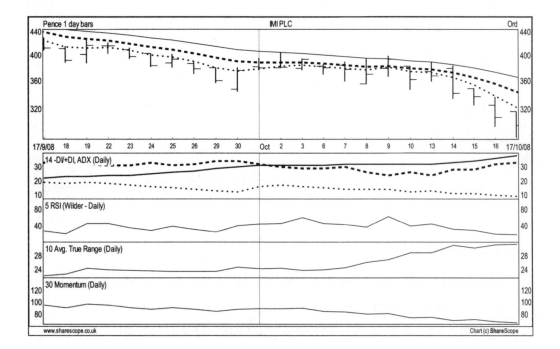

IMI 6

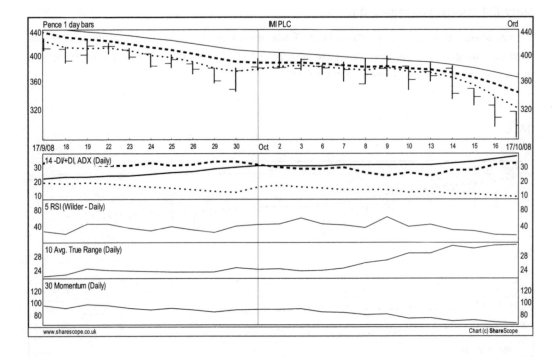

Commentary on this chart:

1. If you used a 1 ATR stop and entered at the first opportunity you went short at 376.25 with a stop at 400.25; the latest close is 297.75 so you are sitting on a profit of over three times your original risk. You need to preserve some of that profit; options include using the latest fractal resistance as a stop, moving the stop to break even, putting a stop above the high of the last 2, 3 or 4 days, trailing an ATR stop from the latest close. Or some combination of these? What do you do when you trade? Which techniques in this book do you feel comfortable using in your exit methodology?

2. Decide where your stop will be before moving on to the next chart (which is ten days forward).

IMI 7

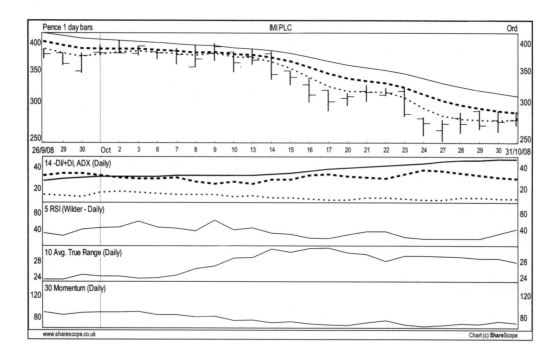

IMI 7

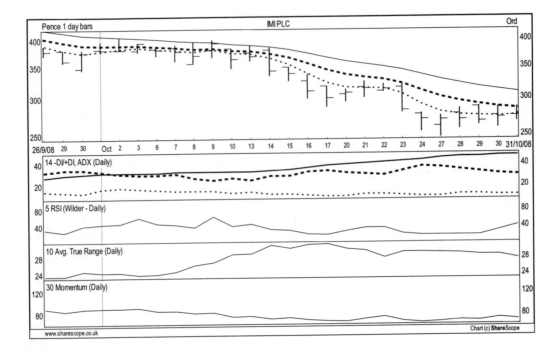

Commentary on this chart:

1. What did you decide about a trailing stop? The latest close is 275p, so with the assumptions we used before the profit is now 4.2 times your initial risk. Many traders will want to lock in a profit of at least two times risk, so the stop needs to be low enough to guarantee this.

2. Have a look at the fractal low on 17 October; now look at the fractal high on 29 October – both at roughly the same level – the support on 17 October has become resistance.

3. My personal preference at this point, given the size of the profit to date, would be to set a tight stop a little above the fractal high of 29 October.

4. A longer-term trader than me would look at the ADX and the moving average combination and wonder why we were even thinking of exiting at this point – the downtrend is still intact!

We move on another day...

IMI 8

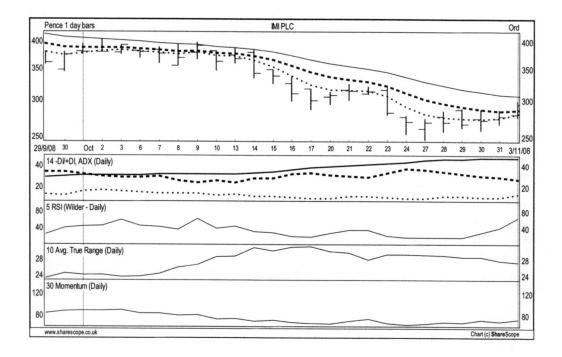

IMI 8

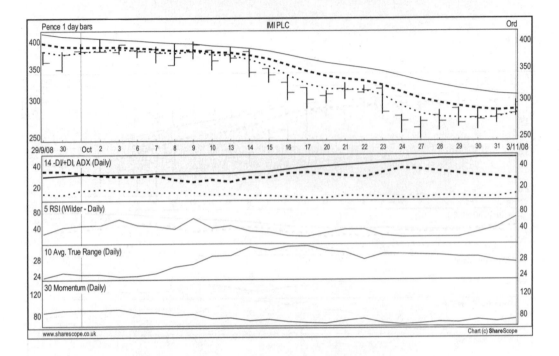

Commentary on this chart:

1. That is me out, that fractal high was penetrated, my stop 3p above it at 288p was hit; the profit at this exit point is 3.7 times the initial risk. At the lowest point in the trade the profit got to be 5.5 times initial risk, and one of my own rules is not to give back more profit than twice the initial risk.

2. Do you have rules for exits covering this trade; have you followed them?

Now we fast forward to the end of December.

I have circled the entry and the exit points for this trade per one set of assumptions above. The chart includes the lowest price this stock reached during the five months after the entry.

Any thoughts?

IMI 9

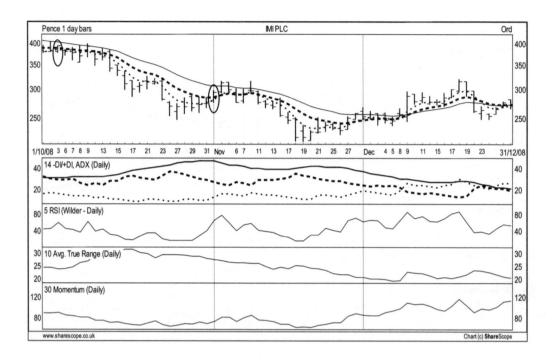

IMI 9

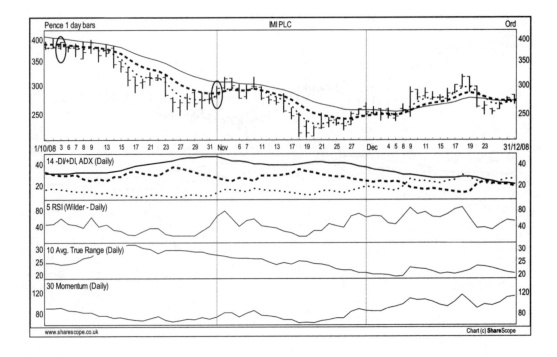

Commentary:

Do you review your trades after you have taken them?

1. It is useful to review trades periodically in a thorough way, to see if there are any learning points. Was the entry well timed? Am I leaving too much on the table by exiting too early? Am I giving up too much profit by exiting too late?

2. There are always trade-offs in trading. For instance if one holds out for more profit one increases the risk of giving back what has already been won.

3. With hindsight it was possible to ride this for one more leg down; at the lowest point it reached the profit would have been 6.8 times the initial risk.

4. One tip: a way to measure the quality of the timing of exits is to look at the amount of profit gained (here 3.7) and compare it to the maximum possible (here 6.8). 54% may or may not be acceptable depending on the trader's time frame, risk preferences, personal style of trading and objectives. And this is just one trade; for meaningful data to be compiled one needs to look at a series of trades.

5. I hope the charts in this chapter have served to pull together some of the themes in this book, and also have begun to illustrate that there is much more to trading success than just indicators. Indicators can assist in both entry and exit methodology, but other factors are critical, including bet size, discipline and psychology.

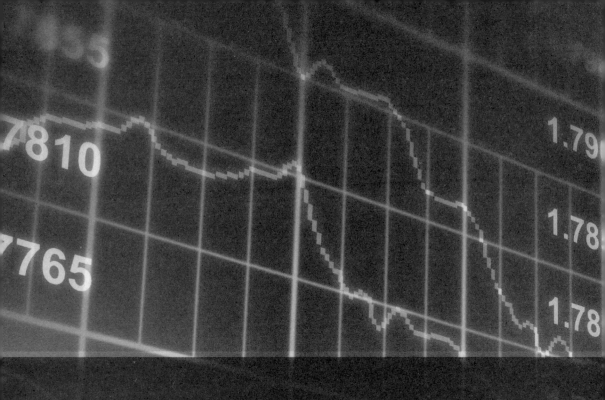

APPENDICES

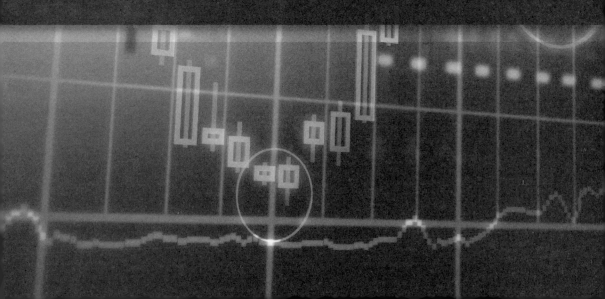

Further Notes on ATR, ADX and Moving Averages

ATR

A measure is taken each period of the distance travelled by price during that period. This is called the *True Range*. Then an average is taken of the True Range over a user-defined number of periods.

For the majority of periods the distance travelled by price during the period is calculated simply as the difference between the highest price and the lowest price in the period.

Gaps

But there is an extra tweak to the calculation which is used when there has been a gap. I define a gap here as when the highest price of a period is lower than the close of the previous period. Or when the lowest price of a period is higher than the close of the previous period. When there has been a gap the measure of the distance travelled by price during the period after the gap is adjusted to incorporate the gap.

More precisely the calculation of ATR is as follows.

First calculate the True Range of each period. The True Range is defined as the largest value of:

- the distance from today's high to today's low

- the distance from yesterday's close to today's high

- the distance from yesterday's close to today's low

Then create a moving average of True Range values over a user-defined number of periods. Welles Wilder in his book did not just total the True Range values and divide by the number of periods; rather, he used formulae to take yesterday's ATR value and then adjust it for today's True Range. Back in those days, before personal computers, this would have been a useful shortcut for traders. These days a computer will calculate ATR for you without you really needing to lift up the bonnet and have a look at the engine; but in any case I don't think it would make a lot of practical difference what type of moving average was used, simple, exponential, weighted, triangular or Welles Wilder's own version.

ADX

The calculations behind the Directional Movement tool are quite complex. Here is a simplified version which captures the essence of the calculations.

1. First, DM is calculated – DM stands for Directional Movement and is the largest part of this period's True Range which is outside of the previous period's True Range. If this is above the previous period's True Range it is labelled +DM; if it is below it is labelled –DM.

2. DM is then divided by the True Range. The precise definition of True Range was given on the previous page.

3. An average is taken of the +DM and –DM values over a user-defined number of periods, and divided by an average of the True Range values over that number of periods, to produce two Directional Movement Indicator values, +DI and –DI. Software plotting the +DI and –DI values usually allow the user to choose different colours or different styles for them: green for +DI and red for –DI is a popular choice.

4. A derivative of +DI and –DI is then calculated, ADX, the Average Directional Movement Index. The sum of all +DI values and all –DI values over a user-defined period is first calculated, then the difference between the two totals is divided by the sum of the two totals and converted to a percentage.

Note that each of +DI, –DI and ADX have a possible range of 0 to 100.

Note also that ADX increases (rises) as a trend develops irrespective of whether the trend is up or down. Think of two extreme cases:

1. in a powerful uptrend where there are no –DI values, only +DI values, ADX will eventually rise to 100, and

2. in a powerful downtrend where there are no +DI values, only –DI values, ADX will also eventually rise to 100.

Moving averages

Some analysts have argued that the most recent price action is more important than older data. Therefore, over the years, other types of moving average have been designed, primarily to give more emphasis to more recent prices. The most important of these is the exponential moving average.

The calculation for an exponential moving average is as follows:

1.   take the previous moving average value and multiply it by a factor

2.   take the most recent price and multiply it by a factor

3.   add the two values together

The factors used are determined by the length of moving average required by the user, and as that required length reduces so the factor applied to the most recent price increases.

Here is a worked example:

A 9 day exponential moving average uses a factor of .8 for the previous moving average value and a factor of .2 for the most recent price. (More on how the factors are determined shortly.)

So if yesterday's 9 day exponential moving average value was 100 and the most recent price is 105 the new 9 day exponential moving average value is calculated as:

(100 x .8) + (105 x .2) = 80 + 21 = 101

The formula for calculating the factor to apply to the latest close (and 1 minus the factor to the latest moving average value) is:

Factor = 2 / (time periods +1)

So in this example of the 9 period exponential moving average the factor is calculated as:

2 / (time periods + 1) = 2 / (9 + 1) = 2/ 10 = 0.2 (as used above)

The practically-oriented trader using exponential moving averages does not need to know the detailed mechanics of how they are constructed since trading software packages do all the calculations behind the scenes. The key thing is that they react to price change more quickly than simple moving averages – as we saw in the chapter on moving averages.

For many traders the choice really lies between simple and exponential moving averages, with perhaps the majority going these days for exponential. However it is worth pointing out that there are a number of other types.

For instance:

- *weighted* – each period in the moving average's timescale is given a weighting which is multiplied by the price in the period, and a higher weighting is applied to more recent periods;

- *triangular* – places more weight on the middle portion of the series of price data;

- *variable* – a type of exponential moving average that varies the weighting of the most recent price as the volatility of the instrument changes; and

- *VIDYA* (short for Variable Index Dynamic Average) – a type of variable moving average.

For those interested in further research on the detailed calculations behind all tools used in this book I recommend *Technical Analysis from A to Z* by Steven Achelis.

Resources

Books

I list below books that I have read and would recommend.

Inter market analysis

John J. Murphy: *Intermarket Analysis: Profiting from Global Market Relationships* (John Wiley & Sons Inc., 2004)

Technical analysis

John J. Murphy: *The Visual Investor: How to Spot Market Trends* (John Wiley & Sons Inc., 1996).

John J. Murphy: *Technical Analysis of the Financial Markets: A Comprehensive Guide to Trading Methods and Applications* (New York Institute of Finance, 1999)

Introductions to trading

Dr. Alexander Elder: *Trading for a Living: Psychology Trading Tactics Money Management* (John Wiley & Sons Inc., 1993)

Dr. Alexander Elder: *Come into my Trading Room: A Complete Guide to Trading* (John Wiley & Sons Inc., 2002)

Developing trading systems

Tushar S. Chande: *Beyond Technical Analysis: How to Develop and Implement a Winning Trading System* (John Wiley & Sons Inc., 2001)

Bruce Babcock Jr.: *The Business One Irwin Guide to Trading Systems* (Business One Irwin, 1989)

Charles Le Beau & David W. Lucas: *Technical Traders Guide to Computer Analysis of the Futures Market* (McGraw-Hill, 1992)

Curtis M. Faith: *Way of the Turtle: The Secret Methods that Turned Ordinary People into Legendary Traders* (McGraw Hill, 2007)

Trading issues such as position sizing

Van K. Tharp: *Trade Your Way to Financial Freedom (Second Edition): – Searching for the Holy Grail in the market – Discovering what makes a trader a winning trader – Managing reward to risk in your trades* (Lake Lucerne Limited Partnership, 2007)

Van K. Tharp: *Van Tharp's Definite Guide to Position Sizing: How to Evaluate your System and Use Position Sizing to Meet your Objectives* (The International Institute for Trading Mastery, 2008)

Psychology and trading

Mark Douglas: *Trading in the Zone: Master the Market with Confidence, Discipline and a Winning Attitude* (New York Institute of Finance, 2000)

Interviews, biographies

Jack D. Schwager: *Market Wizards: Interviews with Top Traders* (Harper Business, 1989)

Jack D. Schwager: *The New Market Wizards: Conversations with America's Top Traders* (Harper Business, 1992)

Jack D. Schwager: *Stock Market Wizards: Interviews with America's Top Stock Traders* (John Wiley & Sons Inc., 2001)

Edwin Lefevre: *Reminiscences of a Stock Market Operator* (John Wiley and Sons, Inc., 1993, originally published in 1923 by George H. Doran and Company)

Specific techniques

J. Welles Wilder Jr.: *New Concepts in Technical Trading Systems* (Trend Research, 1978)

Steve Nison: *Japanese Candlestick Charting Techniques: A Contemporary Guide to the Ancient Investment Techniques of the Far East* (New York Institute of Finance, 2001)

Steve Nison: *Beyond Candlesticks: New Japanese Charting Techniques Revealed* (John Wiley & Sons Inc., 1994)

John Bollinger: *Bollinger on Bollinger Bands* (McGraw-Hill, 2002)

Jeremy du Plessis: *The Definitive Guide to Point and Figure: A Comprehensive Guide to the Theory and Practical Use of the Point and Figure Charting Method* (Harriman House Publishing, 2005)

Richard W. Arms, Jr: *Stop and Make Money: How to Profit in the Stock Market Using Volume and Stop Orders* (John Wiley & Sons Inc., 2008)

Dr Charles B. Schaap: *ADXcellence, Power Trend Strategies* (StockMarketStore.com, 2006)

Setups

David Landry: *Dave Landry on Swing Trading* (M. Gordon Publishing Group, 2002)

Laurence A. Connors & Linda Bradford Raschke: *Street Smarts: High Probability Short-term Trading Strategies* (M. Gordon Publishing Group, 1995)

Websites

Here are some websites to check out.

www.spreadbettingcentral.co.uk

This is the website I edit. Market analysis and regular blogs on a range of spread betting and trading issues. This site provides links to spread betting firms and to sites providing resources for spread betting. There is a forum on this site which any reader of this book is welcome to use to discuss the book or any trading issues of interest.

www.stockcharts.com

A subscription site, but with several useful free areas. In particular the Market Summary in the Free Charts area, and the Chart School, which provides explanations of a range of technical analysis tools.

www.sparkdales.co.uk

Information on training seminars I run.

www.iitm.com

This is the site of Dr Van Tharp, psychologist and trading coach, featured in *Market Wizards* (recommended reading).

www.sharescope.co.uk

This is the site of the provider of the software used to produce all the charts in this book.

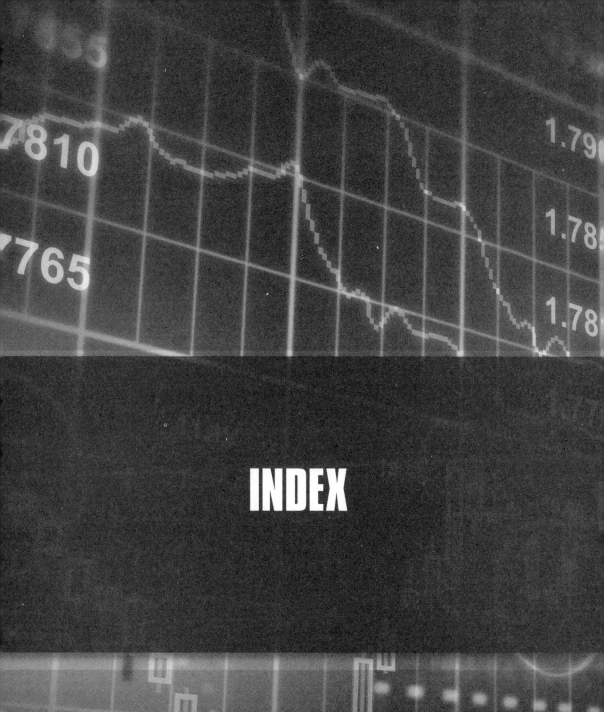

INDEX

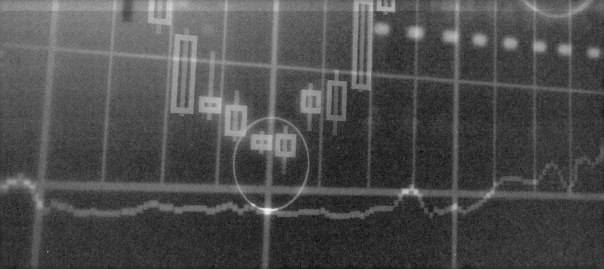

A

Achelis, Steven 142

ADX, see 'directional movement'

Antofagasta, examples of:

oscillators 78

support and resistance 59-61

Aroon indicator 35

ATR 11-22, 139

alternatives to 21-22

background and construction of 11-12

examples 18-20, 104, 127

FTSE 100, example of 11

gaps 139

how to use it 14-22

multiple to use 14-15

overview 13

periods 13, 14, 19-21

risk-reward comparisons 16

settings 13

stops, placing 14-16, 19-20, 128

strengths of 13

time frames 13

volatility 11, 19

visual inspection, 'see visual inspection'

weakness of 13

average true range, see 'ATR'

B

Balfour Beatty, momentum example of 103-109

bearish engulfing pattern 54

bet size 3, 16-17, 19, 20-21, 22, 60, 110, 124, 127, 135

Bollinger, John 43, 144

Bollinger bands 43

BT Group, oscillators example of 81-83

bullish engulfing pattern 54

C

candlestick charts 54

Carpetright PLC, oscillators example of 79-81

case studies 113-135

Chande, Tushar 35

discipline 135

DM, see 'directional movement'

downtrends 19-20

E

Elder, Dr Alexander 30

entry point 16-17

evening star 54

F

Failure Swing, The 76

falling window 54

Fibonacci 55

fractals 5

      case study 126, 128, 130, 132

      momentum 102, 103, 104

      oscillators 78, 79

      support and resistance 56, 57, 59-60, 61, 62, 63, 64, 65, 66

FTSE 350, case study 115-116

FTSE All Share, examples of:

      case study 113-114

      relative strength 92

G

gaps 79-80, 108, 139

gold, examples of:

      ADX 31-33

      moving averages 45-46

H

hammer 54

Hochschild Mining, example of 61-65

I

island reversal 80-81

IMI, case study of 117-134

J

Japanese candlestick charts, see 'candlestick charts'

S